Doing Digital Right

Doing Digital Right

Louis Lamoureux

ISBN: 0998407100
ISBN-13: 9780998407104

Dedication

To Marian, Melanie, Paul, and Carl

Contents

Introduction

In 1994, Jeff Bezos incorporated Amazon. The company started out without any products, processes, or customers. They did not yet know how to source merchandise, store it, offer it to customers, take orders, collect payment, or ship it.

At that time, Walmart was the dominant retail success story—a company that business students learned about, consultants touted, and authors admired. Barely 30 years old, they had grown to a network of over 2,000 stores pulling in more than $80 billion in annual revenue. Walmart was a master of cost management, supply chain efficiency, and merchandising. They were so beloved by customers that their planned entrance into a new city was often heralded by exuberant headlines in local newspapers, like "We're getting our own Walmart!"

Approximately two decades after their founding, Amazon had become more valuable than Walmart. On July 24, 2015, Amazon's market capitalization reached $246 billion, compared to Walmart's $230 billion. That gap continued to swell. By mid-October, 2016, Amazon's market cap was approximately $400 billion, while Walmart's had dropped to $210 billion.

In just twenty-one years, a company that started from nothing beat an established company that had millions of customers, the world's leading supply chain and distribution expertise, and a respected brand.

That an upstart can dislodge an established company is not news; it has been going on since the dawn of business. In fact, that is precisely what Walmart itself did to established retailers a generation earlier. However, generating $400 billion of wealth in an established industry that already has strong players is unprecedented and does raise a few questions: What did Amazon do? How did they do it? Could established retailers at the time have done it?

As for the first two questions, Amazon entered a mature industry—retail—and used new but viable digital technology to make their processes more efficient and the customer's buying process easier. The Internet and e-commerce technologies they capitalized on were a perfect fit for the industry, and they became commercially viable at just the right time for Amazon.

Regarding the third question: Could established retailers have done the same? Established retailers of the day already had all the physical requirements they needed to give them an advantage over an upstart: warehouses, suppliers, inventory control systems, and shipping relationships. It is true that they lacked the digital acumen, but so did Amazon at its founding. As a new startup, Amazon did not yet have either the physical capacity or the digital processes. So, it seems the established players had the advantage but did not embrace the digital processes at the rapid pace that became natural to Amazon.

However, there's a question that's more useful than speculating about how history could have turned out differently: Can today's established businesses leverage emerging digital technologies to be the disruptors rather than the disrupted? For companies that are predominantly physical—those that make, ship, or repair things; move people; provide face-to-face services—the answer is yes. Existing businesses that leverage their relationships and processes and energetically apply new, viable technologies will be the winners.

What occurred in retail was a preview of what is starting to happen in most other physical industries. Retail happened to be the first to be disrupted because the Internet and e-commerce technologies that enabled disruption in retail were ready first. As new technologies become viable, enabling more efficient processes and facilitating the customer journey, the players who apply the technologies most effectively will disrupt additional industries. Technologies are now emerging that are perfect fits for many other industries: robotics for manufacturing, autonomous vehicles for distribution, artificial intelligence for professional services, cloud technology for computer services, and sensors for industrial products.

I wrote this book because these technologies provide a great opportunity to existing companies and their employees, customers, and shareholders. Ignored or mishandled, though, they pose a significant risk. A balance between over-zealous attempts at transformation and "wait and see" lethargy is imperative.

I also wish to dispel misinformation and bad advice I see being handed out. Established companies do not have to change their business model, they do not have to become platforms, and they should not try to emulate Uber and Airbnb. Our economy of providing products and services for money has not transformed into a "sharing" economy, or a "gig" economy, or even a digital economy.

Today's companies must understand the relevant digital technologies, the business outcomes they enable, and how to apply them in the company's industry. There is no choice. Correctly implementing and using emerging technology is what will separate the next success stories from the businesses that find themselves edged out of the market.

This book examines these topics in depth. Part One: Understanding the Digital World, focuses on "things to know," and provides an overview of the current and emerging state of digital technology—how we got here and what we can soon expect. Part Two: How to Thrive in Digital, is more about "things to do," laying out ways to take advantage of technology to win in the new digital world.

What is the value of this book to you? Simple: it is critical for any executive in any function to understand key digital technologies; the way they are evolving; how companies can leverage them to improve products, processes, and the customer journey; and what kind of business outcomes can be derived. All of that, moreover, is useless without knowing how to help your company define its digital vision and how to act on it. This book, in other words, is a primer on doing digital right and thriving in the new digital era. Perhaps there is a $400 billion opportunity in your industry!

Part 1

Understanding the Digital World

A new digital era is emerging, and established companies who embrace digital are poised to win big. Part 1 of this book explores the new era, the driving technologies, and why existing industrial enterprises are best positioned to thrive.

Chapter 1 introduces the framework for business success in the digital world and describes the three digital eras. Chapter 2 looks at companies' business performance relative to the degree of digital initiatives they have undertaken. Chapter 3 describes the digital technologies that took us to 2015— covering the first and second digital eras, and Chapter 4 describes the technologies that will shape the third digital era.

Enough introduction. Let's get started.

One

The Digital World

CONSTANTS AND CHANGES OVER TIME

General Electric (GE) purchased a Univac 1 computer in 1954 to automate payroll and manufacturing in their major appliance manufacturing facility in Louisville, Kentucky. GE had witnessed advances in the world of computer technology and wanted to position itself as a leader in deploying the new technology. Their implementation of the Univac 1 made them the first business to use digital technology in North America.[1]

GE hired Arthur Andersen to help write the program and named Roddy F. Osborne IT project manager, making him the first person to ever hold that title. While the initiative suffered from the first IT project delay and cost overrun, in the end, it was a success.

Fast forward to 2006. In their annual report, GE outlines the fact that their customers are increasingly using the Internet and lays out their vision for capitalizing on digitization by moving online. They discuss setting up online tools for their customers, ranging from decision support systems to help locomotive customers improve fuel efficiency to Web-based electronic medical records. The report also outlines how they originated $4 billion of loans online through GE Money, acquired $4 billion in revenue from digital services, and drove digital process efficiencies to improve margins.[2]

A decade later, in June 2016, GE held a "Digital Investor" meeting with its shareholders. At the meeting, they painted a picture of the rapidly advancing digital world and how they were leveraging technologies such as machine learning, artificial intelligence, internet of things (IoT), and cloud computing for several different business uses, including remote equipment inspections, connecting factories, and rolling out new digital offerings. They explained that these initiatives were producing positive business outcomes, including better customer engagement, substantial additional revenue, and better margins. They estimated the industrial Internet market to be $225 billion by 2020 and expected to capture $15 billion in digital revenue by then.

A CONSTANT FRAMEWORK

One company—and three digital stories that span the time from the very first digital business initiative to the writing of this book. There are fascinating similarities and differences across these three stories and across this timeline. First, let's consider the similarities.

In all three stories, GE is using digital technologies to achieve business outcomes (Figure 1-1).

- In 1954, GE leveraged a Univac computer and primitive programming languages to improve payroll and manufacturing processes to lower cost and reduce shipping errors.
- In 2006, GE increased its online presence to connect better with their customers and make it easier for customers to find and order GE's products, driving revenue in the process.
- In 2016, GE leveraged many sophisticated digital technologies to improve products, processes, and customer experience to improve revenue, margins, and customer engagement.

Figure 1-1: Constant Framework for Digital in Business

Furthermore, in each case, the company acted within the context of a digital vision. In 1954, their vision was for the appliance plant to be as modern and sophisticated as possible. In fact, they even chose a site that would facilitate innovative thinking and new processes. A more traditional industrial spot like New York or Massachusetts would have been the obvious choice, but the very fact that these were traditional industrial areas meant they were prone to doing business as usual. Louisville would allow GE to take a fresh approach.

In 2006, digitization was quickly picking up steam, and they wished to capitalize on it. They saw their customers moving to the Internet and wanted to be there for them.

In 2016, GE's vision was no longer just to meet its customers online, but to be the "World's Premier Digital Industrial Company—transforming industry by connecting the physical and digital." This vision drives their decisions and investments, and the initiatives discussed in that investor meeting are all elements for executing it.

The stories also demonstrate three types of business uses of technologies: improving products, processes, and the customer journey. The first story was about improving processes. The 2006 report talks about process efficiencies and making things easier for customers. The 2016 meeting included process and customer journey improvements as well as plans to embed digital technology into products.

Regardless of the decade, there is a consistent framework in the way businesses successfully use digital technology: formulating a vision to use technologies to make products better, improve processes, and make things easier for the customer, all to generate positive business outcomes. Figure 1-2 presents the framework, which we refer to occasionally throughout the book.

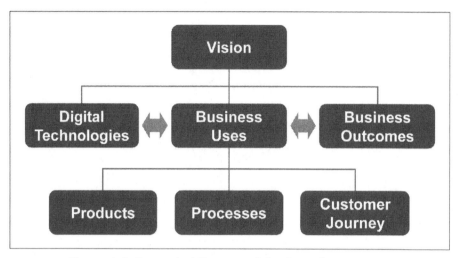

Figure 1-2: Expanded Framework for Digital in Business

Before we proceed any further, please note that I use the word "product" in this book to refer to both products and services, rather than continually stating "products and services." If your company offers services and not tangible products, fear not—this book is for you as well.

MORE TECHNOLOGIES, MORE USES, BIGGER OUTCOMES

We have discussed the constant. Now, let's consider what's different since that early initiative back in 1954. The sophistication and the sheer number of technologies have grown and accelerated in recent years. So has the number of ways to use those technologies. Moreover, the effective application of new technologies is now driving much bigger outcomes.

It is evident that there is far more technology available to us now than in earlier decades. Reviewing the transcript of the 2016 meeting, we can count over 30 technologies that GE is leveraging. In the 1950s, the world was mainly limited to computers and programming languages. After 2000, we added the Internet, mobile phones, and social media. Today, we have all that, plus much more, including the IoT, machine learning, machine vision, robots, robotic process automation, and artificial intelligence.

The following chart presents examples of technologies that companies have leveraged over three different time periods. (The lists across the time periods are not meant to be comprehensive but rather illustrative of the exponential growth.)

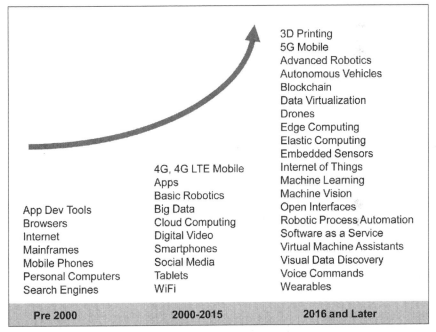

Pre 2000	2000-2015	2016 and Later
		3D Printing
		5G Mobile
		Advanced Robotics
		Autonomous Vehicles
		Blockchain
		Data Virtualization
		Drones
		Edge Computing
		Elastic Computing
		Embedded Sensors
	4G, 4G LTE Mobile	Internet of Things
	Apps	Machine Learning
	Basic Robotics	Machine Vision
App Dev Tools	Big Data	Open Interfaces
Browsers	Cloud Computing	Robotic Process Automation
Internet	Digital Video	Software as a Service
Mainframes	Smartphones	Virtual Machine Assistants
Mobile Phones	Social Media	Visual Data Discovery
Personal Computers	Tablets	Voice Commands
Search Engines	WiFi	Wearables

Figure 1-3: Exponential Increase in Technologies

The range of business uses is also growing exponentially. The following chart lists examples of business uses of new technologies over the three time periods.

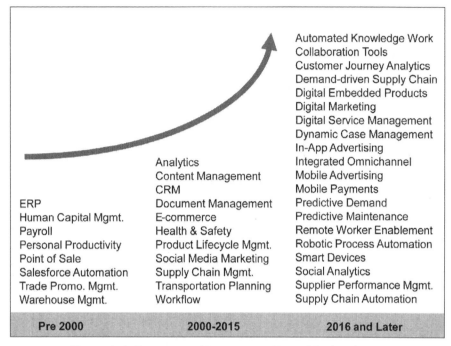

Figure 1-4: Exponential Increase in Use of Technologies

The size of business outcomes is growing rapidly as well. In its 2006 annual report, GE stated they were receiving $4 billion in digital services revenues. Ten years later, in the 2016 meeting, they were targeting $15 billion in digital revenue revenues by 2020 and describing a market size of $225 billion. As digital technology becomes more sophisticated and more of it is available to companies, the payouts that come from using it strategically increase. We saw in the introduction, for example, that Amazon created $400 billion of value by digitizing processes in the traditional industry of retailing.

We will see in Chapter 2 the business results of established companies who are more active in digital initiatives versus those who are less active. The chapter points out that the more digitally active companies added about $1 billion more of value per year than their less active counterparts.

DEFINING DIGITAL

To avoid any confusion, we should lay out a clear definition of "digital." Readers who already know and are comfortable with the concept can skip this section.

The *Merriam-Webster Dictionary* provides a literal definition of "digital" as "anything of, relating to, or being data in the form of binary digits."

Computers understand only binary states—on or off, 1's and 0's—known as a bit (short for binary digits). A single bit can be one of two things: a 1 or a 0. Hence, binary. Two bits can be strung together in four possible combinations (2^2): 0,0; 0,1; 1,0; and 1,1. Eight bits strung together—known as a "byte"—has 2^8, or 256, possibilities. This is enough to represent all the upper-case and lower-case letters in the alphabet, punctuation symbols, and several numbers as well. A five-letter English word, then, requires 5 bytes to represent it. A movie may require about 2 billion bytes, or 2 GB (gigabytes), of storage.

The literal definition is useful, but it does not give us the full picture. "Digital" has come to refer to computing and Internet technology in general. Making a business process digital means using computer and Internet technology to execute that process. When you order something from Amazon, the transaction is entirely digital. A digital product is simply one that is completely based on digital technology, like Google's search engine, for example.

For this book, I define "digital transformation" as "using digital technologies to improve products, processes, or the customer journey." For example, music went through a digital transformation when we moved from storing it on analog media, such as vinyl records, and playing the music on record players, which are physical analog devices, to storing music in digital format on compact discs that are played using CD players. Another transformation occurred when Apple changed our process so that we no longer had to go to a physical store to buy CDs and could instead download music digitally from iTunes.

While we're at it, let's define "physical", since we will be using the word throughout the book: quite simply, matter and movement—things you can see and move.

THREE DIGITAL ERAS

It is my contention that we have been through two digital eras and that we are transitioning into a third. For the sake of brevity, let's call these eras "First Digital," "Second Digital," and "Third Digital." Figure 1-5 outlines each period, along with their technologies and uses, as well as the corresponding product, process, and customer-journey improvements.

	First Digital	Second Digital	Third Digital
Key Technologies	• Mainframes • Programming Languages • Commercial Software • Personal Computers	• Social • Mobile • Analytics • Cloud	• Internet of Things • Machine Learning • Natural Language Processing • Machine Vision • Robotics
Business Uses (Product, Process, Customer)	• Management and Transaction Systems • Personal Productivity	• E-commerce • Mobile Commerce • Online Presence • Analytics • Customer Apps	• Automation of Physical Processes • Automation of Clerical Processes • Digital-Embedded Products • Connected Products • Predictive Analytics • Improved Customer Journey
Business Outcomes	• Efficiencies	• Revenue Protection • Profitability Improvements • Market Valuation Increases	• Better Products Driving More Revenue • Cost Reductions • Improved Customer Loyalty • Market Valuation Increases
	Pre 2000	2000-2015	2016 and Later

Figure 1-5: Three Digital Eras

The dates in Figure 1-5, and those described below, are of course not hard dates where the door closed on one era and opened on the next. Rather, First Digital gradually grew into Second Digital, which has provided the basis for the gradual emergence of Third Digital. Let's take a closer look at each of these eras.

First Digital

First Digital started at the dawn of digital technology in business (around 1954) when enterprises began automating. This period lasted up until the time when the Internet started to become a dominant force (around 2000).

For the first few decades, the technologies were mainframe computers and programming languages for companies to build their own software applications. Commercial software became available in the seventies, and personal computers became mainstream in the eighties. The Internet started to gain steam in the nineties, but did not become a dominant force until Second Digital.

Over this 45-year span, companies automated management and transaction processes like payroll, manufacturing, shipping, order management, accounts receivable, accounts payable, and accounting. Personal computers ushered in personal productivity tools like word processing, spreadsheets, and email.

The business outcomes during this era were primarily efficiencies. For example, manufacturers could operate with less inventory, and all companies could process payroll, invoices, and financial reports with fewer people.

Technology companies such as IBM, Hewlett-Packard, Intel, Microsoft, and Apple came of age. Companies, rather than individuals, were the primary users of the technologies.

Second Digital

Second Digital (2000-2015) was characterized by technologies such as social, mobile, analytics/big data, and cloud applications (including e-commerce)—abbreviated with the acronym "SMAC." The Internet exploded, and new Internet technology providers burst on to the scene with digital products that helped connect people (Facebook), search the Internet (Google), and make it easier to get things (Amazon). Existing companies established their online, e-commerce, and mobile presence. They also started generating massive amounts of data, which they analyzed for deeper insights.

Consumers went online to connect with each other and to access information and entertainment. Companies invested in e-commerce and mobile apps to be where their customers were. Unlike First Digital, both established companies and consumers were using the technologies, with consumers often leading the way.

The business outcome for companies that went online and mobile was, basically, staying in business. Surviving in Second Digital and keeping market share required going to the Internet because that is where the customers were. As we will see in Chapter 2, companies that did it more aggressively tended to have higher profitability and market cap growth than those that were slower to adapt.

Customers came to expect outstanding, beautifully designed products and services that they could purchase with ease. They also grew to expect companies to be always accessible and to help the customer be successful in their use of the products and services. Employees no longer anticipated staying with one employer for their entire careers. Increasingly, they stayed if they wanted to work, the work was enjoyable, and the organization's values matched their own. They also became more likely to provide their time, services, and intelligence on a contract basis, rather than as employees. These expectations and behaviors were formed in Second Digital, but they continue during the next era—Third Digital.

Third Digital
Third Digital Overview
The Third Digital era is upon us. Five key technologies are driving this era: internet of things, machine learning, Natural language processing (NLP), machine vision, and robotics. These are technologies that monitor, learn, listen, see, and move. Several—machine learning, machine vision, and NLP—are forms of artificial intelligence. While the use of Third Digital technologies started to burgeon around 2015, they have been around in less advanced forms for some time. For example, the automotive industry has been leveraging robotics for many years. So, Third Digital has been building for some time.

As pointed out earlier in this chapter, there is a plethora of other technologies available to use, including 3D printing, blockchain, wearables, and nanobots. However, I believe these other technologies will not have as big or as near-term an impact on business as the first five.

Businesses use these five key technologies to revolutionize products, processes, and customer journeys in several ways. First, the technologies allow physical processes to be automated that previously were unsuccessful in doing so. Today, robots can load pallets or trucks with boxes of odd sizes and different weights, assemble consumer electronics, sew garments, prepare meals, make coffee, deliver room service, and kill terrorists.

Through a field called robotic process automation (RPA), these technologies can also automate back office or administrative processes like invoice processing, job applicant screening, customer record updates, claims processing, and purchase requisitions.

Other uses include embedding digital technologies into products to make them smarter, connected, and more reliable; sifting through vast amounts of data for insights and predictions; and improving customer outcomes by helping them use products more effectively.

Business outcomes include new revenue streams, improved customer journeys, and significant reductions in costs. The companies who apply the technologies most effectively will restructure their industries—the way Amazon restructured retail.

Third Digital includes three interesting characteristics: big data getting bigger; fusing of physical and digital; and companies becoming providers, not just users, of digital.

Big Data Gets Bigger

Second Digital initiated the creation and analysis of large amounts of data. Third Digital explodes that further. The reason for embedding products with digital technology is to create and analyze data. Previously, most data was generated by transactions. Now data is being continually created without transactions taking place. Not only is the volume of data exploding, but the types and varieties are as well. Companies are looking for and analyzing unstructured data from text, video, and audio.

Digital Plus Physical

An aspect of Third Digital is the fusing of digital and physical. In the first and second eras, physical was mostly separate from digital. On the physical side, people loaded trucks; doctors performed diagnoses; drivers drove cars and trucks; workers operated tractors—all without much assistance from computers. Of course, there were exceptions. Robotics, for example, has been deployed for many years in factories, but the technologies, until now, have not been sufficiently advanced to pervade our everyday lives. On the digital side, the leading digital applications, including social networks, blogging tools, and search engines, were digital-only products.

However, digital is now being embedded into physical products, from sports equipment to industrial machines, to make them smarter and more connected. Most industrial assets now go beyond performing their tasks; they generate data and insights about the asset itself. Companies are automating physical processes.

These trends are good news for established industrial companies whose product has, for decades, been physical. Businesses that manufacture machines, air conditioning units, vehicles, furniture, food, energy, clothing, or pharmaceuticals, or provide services like health care, transportation, courier, or electrical devices, know how to produce and sell these physical products. They certainly know it better than any upstart would. Their new task is to be leaders in adding digital processes to their businesses and embedding digital into their products.

Users Become Providers

Established companies will not only be users of digital technology; the successful ones will become providers of it as well. They will embed digital into their products and provide digital-only offerings, such as software and information. The chart below outlines examples of digital providers and users over the three eras.

	First Digital	Second Digital	Third Digital
Primary Providers of Digital	Tech companies, like • IBM • Intel • Microsoft • Apple • Dell	First Digital companies, plus internet, device and e-commerce companies, like • Facebook • Google • Apple • Amazon	Second Digital companies, plus digital product and service providers, like • Tesla • GE • Established companies
Primary Users of Digital	• Established companies	• Consumers	• Established companies • Consumers

Figure 1-6: Digital Providers

Staying with the GE example, an increasing portion of GE's revenue is coming from the digital products and services that they provide. Its Predix offering, which is a set of software and systems for connecting equipment and creating and analyzing data to help industrial customers improve efficiencies, generated $7 billion in revenue in 2016 and GE expects it to generate $15 billion in 2020.

CONCLUSION

The number and complexity of useful digital technologies are increasing exponentially. Managers know their companies need to invest in digital technologies. However, in the world of finite resources in which we all live, decisions to proceed with digital investments force decisions to not proceed with other investments, such as plant expansions, marketing campaigns, geographic expansion, and acquisitions. Therefore, some assessment of financial returns associated with digital initiatives is required. That is the purpose of the next chapter.

Two

Digital and Corporate Performance

STUDY APPROACH

Since you are reading this book, you are probably not skeptical about the large threat and opportunity that digital presents. However, you do have a right to ask about numbers. Sure, everyone knows about the stories like Amazon generating $400 billion in wealth, but everyone also knows that these are long shots. What about "regular" companies undertaking digital initiatives? Any data there?

While there isn't any empirical data indicating that $X invested in digital initiatives generates $Y in value, we can nevertheless look at the available information and make judgments about the value of digital initiatives. Specifically: Are the companies that are actively engaging in digital initiatives performing better than companies who are less active?

This chapter addresses the business outcomes of digital initiatives (Figure 2-1).

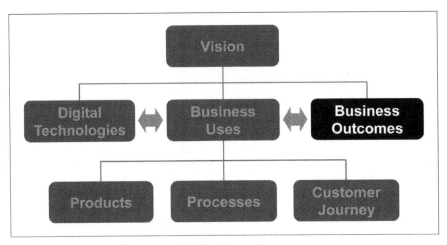

Figure 2-1: Business Outcomes

For this book, I worked with a research team to examine the degree to which companies have undertaken digital initiatives over the last five years and to investigate whether there is any correlation between those initiatives and business performance. We wanted the research to be easily replicable over time in order to have the option to update the findings annually. For that reason, we only studied publicly available information that we can keep accessing from year to year. As such, the team examined publicly traded companies.

We started with companies in the Standard & Poor's (S&P) 500 index. We added the 20 largest companies on the Toronto Stock Exchange to get some Canadian representation. We planned to examine five years of annual reports (2011 through 2015), so we narrowed the list of companies to those for which we could obtain annual reports for at least four of the five years. That left us with 449 companies out of the original 520.

The list below shows the industries represented and the number of companies examined in each industry. (See the Appendix for the full list of companies.)

- Banks: 25
- Biotech and Pharma: 13
- Broadcasting and Communications: 16
- Consumer Discretionary: 27
- Consumer Packaged Goods: 28
- Diversified Financial Services: 20
- Health Care Equipment & Distribution: 22
- Health Care Providers: 13
- Industrials: 68
- Information Technology: 44
- Insurance: 19
- Internet Commerce and Services: 19
- Materials: 22
- Oil & Gas: 39
- Real Estate and REITs: 18
- Retail: 28
- Utilities: 27
- Total: 448

METHODOLOGY

To identify the extent to which each company was undertaking digital initiatives, we examined annual reports for mentions of words associated with such initiatives and activities. This research was conducted in a manner akin to sentiment analysis, which corporations undertake to learn what customers are saying about them. We took the number of mentions as an indication of the company's digital activity. After all, if the chairman or CEO is commenting on a digital initiative in their letter in the annual report, it is safe to assume that the initiative is important to them.

In fact, analyzing the CEO or chairman's letter or other narrative content in annual reports has been proven to provide useful information and even accurate predictions. A 1997 study by professors Rodney K. Rogers and Julia Grant concluded that the narrative sections of annual reports provide twice as much information as the financial statements.[1] In 2000, Professors Malcolm Smith and Richard Taffler studied the concept further and concluded that the narrative in a chairman's letter "permits a high degree of discrimination in the classification of bankrupt and financially healthy firms." They determined that analyzing seven keywords enabled them to classify the financial health 98% of the time.[2] So, words in the annual reports do matter.

For this book, we looked for ten keywords typically associated with digital initiatives:

- Analytics
- App
- Big Data
- Cloud
- Digital
- Internet of Things
- Mobile
- Robotics, Robots
- Sensor
- Social Media

We started with a longer list that included such words as "wearables," "drones," "nanobots," "3D printing," but those words did not appear frequently enough to be statistically significant.

We also examined the context to ensure the sentence did, in fact, indicate a digital initiative. For example, a sentence discussing "mobile oil rigs" did not get counted as a mention of a mobile digital initiative.

We quickly realized that it is not useful to mix primarily digital companies with companies whose products and processes are mainly physical in nature. Clearly, businesses like Amazon, Yahoo, and IBM will have far more mentions of digital keywords than companies like General Mills, Boeing, and 3M.

The total number of mentions over the five years were orders of magnitude greater in the three technology industries: Information Technology, Broadcasting and Communications, and Internet Commerce and Services than in the non-technology industries. Therefore, for the bulk of the analysis, we eliminated these outliers by removing the technology companies from consideration.

Of course, the presence of digital words, even within context, is not a fully accurate representation of digital initiatives. Companies may undertake digital initiatives and not mention them in their annual reports. We believe, however, that it is a close enough approximation to gauge the degree of digital activity across various business sectors.

The following examples of mentions provide a deeper understanding of the approach we used. They also provide examples of digital initiatives that companies are undertaking (mentions of keywords are in italics for clarity).

Analytics

Manulife (2015): "The U.S. Division invested in advanced *analytics* to modernize the purchase process and to better understand customer and distribution needs to provide a better customer experience."

General Electric (2014): "We are launching game-changing applications to improve our efficiency. An example is our Brilliant Factory initiative where we are unleashing the power of *analytics* in our manufacturing plants."

App

JPMorgan Chase (2015): "We added new functionality to our mobile *app* with account preview and check viewing, and we redesigned *chase.com* with simpler navigation and more personalized experiences, making it easier for our customers to bank and interact with us when and how they want—via smartphones, laptops and other mobile devices. We now have nearly 23 million active Chase mobile customers, a 20% increase over the prior year."

Costco (2014): "This year we improved the navigation, checkout performance and search engine optimization of our websites. We also relaunched our mobile site and *apps* for smartphones and tablets."

Big Data

Caterpillar (2015): "We are harnessing the power of *big data* to offer our customers insights that decrease operating costs, increase uptime and maximize profitability. In the process, we're shaping a new era for Caterpillar in which we not only manufacture machines and engines but also deliver value-added solutions."

American Express (2015): "Our focus on costs also involves spending our investment dollars more efficiently. We'll continue to use *big data analytics* to improve the way we evaluate, prioritize and execute our investment opportunities."

Cloud

General Electric (2014): "We are putting 70% of our applications on the *cloud* to improve flexibility."

Marsh & McLennan (2014): "Our mobile, *cloud-based risk management* platform is helping to move the market in an entirely new direction."

Digital

Black & Decker (2015): "*Digital Excellence* means leveraging the power of emerging technologies across the company's businesses to connected devices, the internet of things, and big data, as well as social and mobile."

Under Armour (2014): "Our Connected Fitness strategy is focused on connecting with our consumers. We plan to engage and grow this community by developing innovative applications, services and other *digital* solutions to impact how athletes and fitness-minded individuals train, perform, and live."

Internet of Things

Parker Hannifin (2015): "Our services strategy will center on the significant potential offered by the *internet of things (IoT)* as we expand the use of our Web-enabled solutions across our broad technology platform to better serve our customers by improving uptime, reducing safety risks, and optimizing processes."

Tyco (2014): "When we launched the new Tyco, we began investing in our *internet of things* platform. We recognized trends in sensors and networks, and made sure that we were developing intelligent edge devices to provide visibility to assets, people, and the environment."

Mobile

Assurant (2014): "With a comprehensive array of *mobile* and extended warranty programs for smartphones, appliances, consumer electronics and other devices, we see many opportunities to serve the rapidly expanding base of connected consumers."

Cigna (2014): "… make health management more interesting by combining our health coaches, *mobile applications*, social media and games to help customers and their families evaluate their health, find tools to improve their health, track their progress, and earn rewards."

Robotics, Robots

Royal Caribbean Cruises (2015): "We were the first at sea to offer *robotic* bartenders."

Charles Schwab (2015): "A *'robo-advisor'* offers a user-friendly website and mobile experience where an investor can answer a few questions, have a complete investment portfolio built, and receive ongoing management with rebalancing."

Sensor

PPL Corporation (2015): "We're incorporating new *sensors*, automation and technology that allow us to quickly restore power to many customers before we even dispatch crews to trouble spots."

FedEx (2013): "Leading the way in *sensor*-based logistics is SenseAware®, a small multi-sensor device that can sense and transmit data about six key shipment variables: temperature, light exposure, humidity, barometric pressure, shock and location."

Social Media

Estée Lauder (2015): "Initiatives include collaborating with Millennial influencers around the world, producing branded content across their *social media platforms* and introducing Kendall Jenner as a new spokesmodel."

Starbucks (2012): "We are further translating our connective spirit be-yond the walls of our stores by leveraging a combination of *social and digital media*. It is hard to overstate the collective power of Starbucks', 54 million Facebook fans, 3 million Twitter followers, and 14.6 million loyalty program members."

With that background to the study, let's look at the results.

VOLUME OF DIGITAL ACTIVITY

Before examining the relationship between digital activity and business performance, let's look at the volume of digital activity over time. The following chart (Figure 2-2) shows the number mentions for the 369 non-tech companies over the five-year period. Mentions of digital keywords doubled over the five years and increased by a whopping 27% in the most recent year. So, the number of mentions is not only increasing, but accelerating, indicating that companies are undertaking more and more digital initiatives.

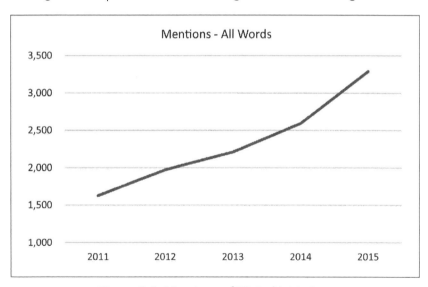

Figure 2-2: Mentions of Digital Initiatives

We can also look at the number of mentions for each word. Because the number of mentions varies significantly by word, and because we wanted to ensure readability, we spread the ten keywords across three graphs (Figures 2-3, 2-4, and 2-5). Note that the vertical scale varies significantly in each graph.

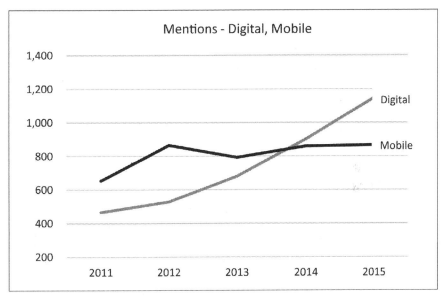

Figure 2-3: Mentions of Digital and Mobile

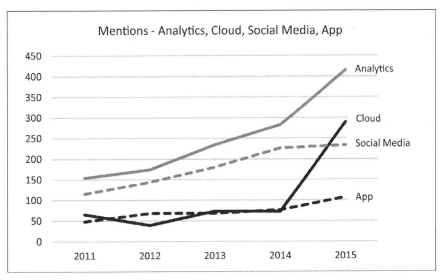

Figure 2-4: Mentions of Analytics, Cloud, Social Media, and App

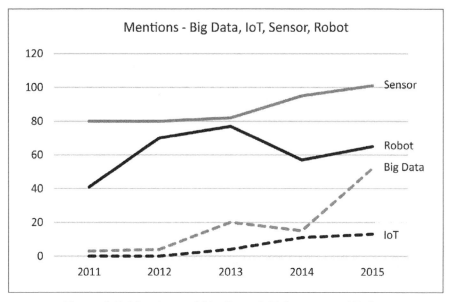

Figure 2-5: Mentions of Big Data, IoT, Sensor, and Robot

A few interesting observations:

- The largest absolute growth was in the use of "digital," which was mentioned 800 times more in 2015 than it had been in 2011.
- There are also rapid increases in the words "analytics," "cloud," and "big data." The number of initiatives in these areas is growing rapidly.
- While the frequency of most words is increasing, mention of the word "mobile" plateaued in 2012.

RELATIONSHIP TO BUSINESS PERFORMANCE

Key Metrics

The next step was to analyze whether companies that are more actively employing digital technology tend to enjoy better business performance. We measured business performance according to five indicators:

- Market capitalization growth
- Revenue growth
- Net income improvement
- Earnings before interest, tax, depreciation and amortization (EBITDA) improvement
- Return on assets (ROA) improvement

Using these five measures gives us a picture of performance that blends company value growth (market capitalization), sales increases (revenue), profitability (net income, EBITDA), and asset utilization (ROA).

Rather than looking at the static measures, we looked at the growth and improvement of these metrics over time. For example, a company's absolute market capitalization was of little interest, while its increase in market capitalization was much more important. This approach allowed us to see whether companies were experiencing improvements over time, regardless of their starting point.

We sorted the 369 non-tech companies according to how many mentions of the digital words existed in the five years of annual reports. At the bottom was zero—companies who had no mentions, and at the top were companies with more than 100 mentions. We then put the companies into two lists—top half (companies with more than the median number of mentions) and bottom half (companies with fewer than the median number of mentions).

We examined the business performance of the companies in each half with two questions in mind:

1. Did the companies with more mentions outperform those with fewer mentions?
2. Did companies with more mentions outperform those with fewer *relative to* the average for that company's industry?

Question 2 allows us to ensure that the comparisons we make are relevant within an industry. Take Dollar General, for example. Their average market cap growth rate was 14.1% per year. It is challenging to tell with that figure alone just how well they are performing. We get a much better idea of this when we compare that level of growth with the average growth for all the companies examined in the retail industry, which was 18.7% per year. So, Dollar General's growth *relative* to their industry was 14.1%–18.7% = -4.6%, meaning that its market cap growth, while positive, is below the industry average.

Table 2-1 summarizes the results for the two questions:

	1: Performance for companies with higher mentions is:	2. Performance for companies with higher mentions, relative to industry, is:
Market Cap Growth	Higher	Higher
Revenue Growth	No Difference	No Difference
Net Income Margin Growth	Higher	Higher
EBITDA Margin Growth	Higher	Higher
Return on Assets Growth	Higher	No Difference

Table 2-1: Summary of Business Outcomes Relative to Mentions of Digital Initiatives

So, companies more active in digital transformation show better results than less active companies in valuation, profitability, and asset utilization. Interestingly, the more digitally active companies are not yet showing better revenue growth. We can speculate on why this is, but that is what it would be—speculation. We do anticipate that in Third Digital, more active companies will indeed enjoy more revenue growth as products and services become more digitized.

While no methodology is capable of isolating and quantifying the impact of digital initiatives and revealing a strong statistical relationship, the top half/bottom half approach is a useful way to summarize this relationship. Note also that this is simply data and relationships. As every analyst knows, correlation is not causation: we cannot demonstrate that embracing digital initiatives *causes* better performance. However, we can confidently state that companies more active in digital transformation are performing better than less active companies. Those with more mentions had higher business performance on every measure, except revenue growth.

Let's look at the details. For each measure, we present two charts:

- Performance for top half and bottom half
- Performance relative to industry for the top half and bottom half

As a side note, we also analyzed more finely by looking at quartiles, rather than just top half and bottom half. While more detailed, the conclusions are the same, so we do not present those charts in the book. If you would like to see the more detailed charts, they are available for download at *www.thirddigital.com*.

Market Capitalization Growth

Market capitalization—the stock price multiplied by the total number of outstanding shares—is a tremendously useful measure of the overall value of the company. As the Market Cap Growth chart (Figure 2-6) shows, companies more active in digital transformation have experienced more growth in market cap. Companies in the top half of mentions enjoyed market cap growth of approximately 18% per year versus companies in the bottom half at about 12% per year. Looking at dollars rather than percentages reveals that companies with more mentions grew their market cap at about $4.25 billion per year, versus companies with fewer mentions at $3 billion per year—that is, $1.25 billion more for top half companies. To most people, $1 billion is a lot of money!

The Market Cap Growth Relative to Industry graphic (Figure 2-6) shows that even after removing the effects of industry growth rate, more mentions are still associated with higher market cap growth. Companies in the bottom half of mentions grew market cap more slowly relative to their industry peers.

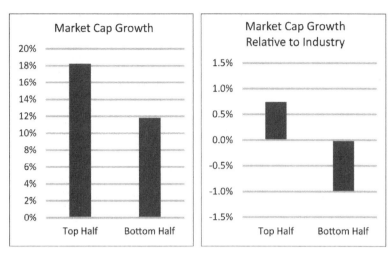

Figure 2-6: Market Cap Growth

Revenue Growth

We did not see a significant difference between top half and bottom in the area of revenue growth. As the charts below show (Figure 2-7), the bottom half has very slightly lower revenue growth, but not enough to be significant. Regarding revenue growth relative to the industry, both halves show no significant movement.

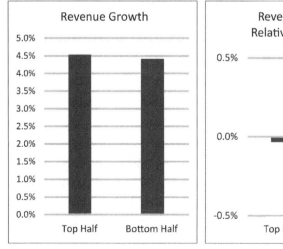
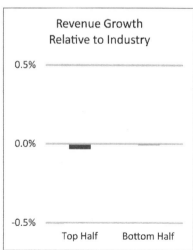

Figure 2-7: Revenue Growth

Net Income Margin Growth

Net income margin is the profit expressed as a percent of revenue. Here, we look at the increase in percentage points—the arithmetic difference between the two percentages. So, if a company's net income margin in 2015 was 5.7% and in 2014 was 5.1%, their points increase in 2015 was 0.6.

Overall, net income margin has gone down. However, companies with higher mentions experienced less of a reduction than companies with fewer mentions, indicating that digital transformation may have helped to inoculate them against industry-wide reductions in net income margin. We see similar results relative to the industry. In fact, the top half improved their next income, while the bottom half saw reductions in net income relative to industry peers (Figure 2-8).

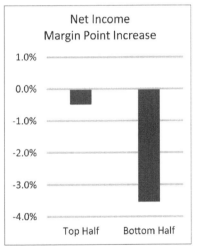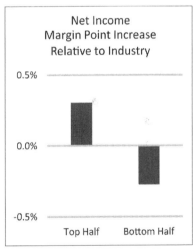

Figure 2-8: Net Income Margin Growth

EBITDA Margin Growth

EBITDA is calculated by taking net income and adding back in the company's interest, taxes, depreciation, and amortization expenses. The measure gives an assessment of the company's operating profitability before taking into consideration its non-operating and non-cash expenses.

Like net income growth, we focus on the "percentage points" increase, meaning that, for example, growing from 10.0% to 10.4% is an increase of 0.4 points.

Generally, over the period in question, EBITDA has gone down for the companies evaluated. However, like net income, the reduction was less pronounced for the companies with higher mentions. In fact, the top half almost stayed even, while the bottom half lost an average of three points per year. Relative to industry, the EBITDA point growth is slightly better for companies with more mentions (Figure 2-9).

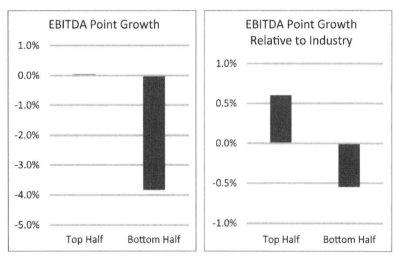

Figure 2-9: EBITDA Point Growth

Return on Assets (ROA) Growth

ROA is the ratio of net income to the average total assets, expressed as a percentage. It is a good measure of how effectively a company earns a return on its investment in assets. Improving the net income or reducing the amount of assets improves the ratio.

Like the other measures that are expressed as percentages (net income margin and EBITDA), we are interested in the growth of points over time. So improving from 5.1% to 5.3%, for example, registers as an increase of 0.2 points.

Like net income and EBITDA, ROA has, on average, gone down over the last few years. However, the data shows that the reduction was far less drastic for companies with high mentions than for those with lower mentions. Comparing ROA relative to industry peers reveals that there is no significant difference between companies with high mentions and those with low mentions (Figure 2-10).

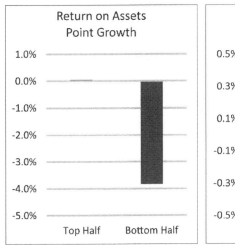 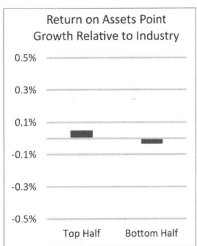

Figure 2-10: Return on Assets Growth

Relationship to Business Performance—Industries

We also looked at the *industry averages* for number of mentions versus market cap growth. We selected market cap growth as the most important single measure, as it represents the market's value of the company, which tends to incorporate all other performance indicators. The following scatter plot (Figure 2-11) shows an interesting result. Except for two outlying industries (Banks and Biotech & Pharma), the remaining 12 industries fit within an area that slopes up and to the right. This visual representation of the data shows us a correlation: higher mentions = higher market cap growth for entire industries. Depending on your industry, you may have to be more digitally active to keep up or exceed your industry peers.

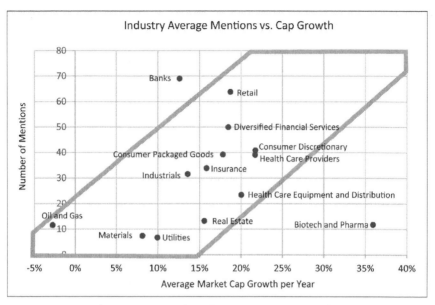

Figure 2-11: Market Cap Growth Relative to Mentions of Digital Initiatives

CONCLUSION

The volume of digital activities is undeniably increasing. Moreover, the data shows that companies that are more active in digital initiatives tend to enjoy better growth in key measures, even after accounting for industry average increases or reductions.

We also see a general trend with entire industries: more digital transformation activity is associated with higher market cap growth. Even in some of the less digitally oriented industries, such as Oil & Gas and Materials, investing in these initiatives makes a difference in business performance.

The analysis in this chapter outlined the results for Second Digital, since we are only now entering Third Digital. As we repeat the study in coming years, the returns are likely to be even higher.

Let's now look at the key technologies that drove the first two digital eras (Chapter 3) and that will drive the third era (Chapter 4).

Three

Key Technologies—First and Second Digital

Any manager in any function now needs to understand the fundamental technologies that are driving the digital world. This chapter provides an overview of the technologies involved in the first and second digital eras. This chapter and the next one deal with the technologies portion of the framework (Figure 3-1).

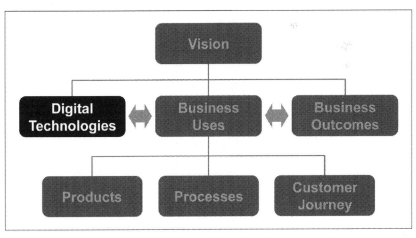

Figure 3-1: Digital Technologies

FIRST DIGITAL TECHNOLOGIES

Other than for its historical value, there isn't much reason to spend a lot of time on First Digital technologies. Many of them are no longer in use, and the ones that are have become so pervasive and commonplace that managers do not need to understand much about them. Still, we will not skip over them because a quick overview is useful to understand the context from which Second Digital and Third Digital technologies have emerged.

Recall that the first digital era spanned the time from the beginning of digital computing in business, around 1954, to circa 2000. Commercial mainframes based on vacuum tubes were sold in the fifties. The tubes supplied binary data: a 1 or 0 depending on whether it was on or off. The invention of the transistor led to much smaller and more reliable computers in the sixties. Punched cards were used to enter data or code, and they eventually gave way to online terminals. Programming languages became more advanced, and databases enabled separation of data from the application. Arpanet, the precursor to the Internet, was established in 1969.

Integrated circuits combining several transistors and computer components onto a single chip enabled more powerful and much smaller computers in the seventies. This development led to the introduction of commercial personal computers in the early eighties and, along with them, the success of companies like Microsoft and Apple. People loved having the power of a full computer on their desks, enabling them to create documents and spreadsheets with greater ease than ever before. At the same time, cell phones were emerging and becoming one of the necessary tools for doing business.

In 1992, Congress allowed commercial activity on the Internet, and the Internet became widely available through user-friendly browsers that allowed people to access it more easily. Search engines brought information to Internet users' fingertips. However, only 7% of the American population was on the Internet in 1999: it was not until 2000 and the second digital era that the Internet emerged as a business tool.

SECOND DIGITAL TECHNOLOGIES

To understand Second Digital technologies, let's first look at a company that leveraged them to great success. In September 2016, JPMorgan Chase surpassed Wells Fargo as the world's largest bank by market capitalization. This accomplishment happens to follow years of aggressively embracing social, mobile, analytics, and cloud technologies. In fact, looking at the research from Chapter 2, they mention those four words—"social", "mobile", "analytics", and "cloud"—more than any other non-technical company. Let's look at their journey.

Although they had a social media misstep in 2013 when they asked Twitter followers to submit questions and had to shut it down within six hours after receiving mostly embarrassing questions such as "Can I get my house back?", since then they have been aggressively using social media effectively. They use Twitter to respond to inquiries and offer solutions to complaints; their Instagram account for investment banking has over 20,000 followers; and they utilize Snapchat to inspire graduates to think about a career with them.

JPMorgan Chase is a leader in mobile banking, counting over 25 million mobile banking users—more than any other bank. The mobile technology not only pleases the customers but improves the bank's profitability since mobile banking costs the bank far less than in-branch banking.

The bank has also become a leader in analytics. In fact, leveraging the analytical capability, the bank has launched a global think tank to analyze their troves of big data and to make their findings and insights available to the public. They have issued such reports as "Insights from 16 Billion Transactions" and "How Falling Gas Prices Fuel the Consumer — Evidence from 25 Million People."

While most banks are reluctant to embrace cloud computing (except for typical applications like Salesforce), JPMorgan Chase is pursuing the cloud aggressively—they recently created the position of "CIO of Cloud Computing" that reports into the global CIO. They are moving much of their infrastructure to the cloud so that their Information Technology function (that includes approximately 19,000 developers) can focus less on servers and networks and more on creating differentiating software. They are also leveraging startup financial technology companies, most of whom offer only cloud-based solutions.[1]

It turns out JPMorgan Chase embraced the technologies that shaped Second Digital: social, mobile, analytics, and cloud computing. During Second Digital, people got connected through social media, and smartphones took our Internet use mobile. Second Digital also ushered in big data/analytics and cloud computing. These technologies, combined, formed the digital backdrop that created the business and social world as we know it today. Also, although Third Digital is emerging with its own set of technologies, they are built on the backs of these four Second Digital technologies. The four technologies will forever be part of the business world, so it is critical to understand them. Let's examine each.

Social and Mobile

We can look at social and mobile together because they are completely intertwined.

Of the world's 7.4 billion people, 2.3 billion are active on social media and 3.8 billion are active mobile users. Two billion people use social media on mobile devices, and that number is growing at a rate of 17% per year (Table 3-1).

	Number (billions)	% of World Population	Growth Rate per Year
World Population	7.4	100%	1%
Active Internet Users	3.4	46%	10%
Active Social Media Users	2.3	31%	10%
Unique Mobile Users	3.8	51%	4%
Active Mobile Social Users	2.0	27%	17%

Table 3-1. Global Internet, Social, and Mobile Activity

If we look at figures for the USA alone, we see even higher penetration percentages. For instance, 87% of the American population regularly use the Internet, 81% use mobile phones, and over half actively use social media on mobile devices.

With respect to devices in the USA, 65% of page views are on desktops and laptops, 27% on mobile phones, and 8% on tablets. The percentage for mobile phones continues to increase rapidly while the other categories are shrinking. Soon, most Internet page views will be from phones. So, any page that your customers see must be set up so that it displays correctly on mobile-sized screens.

Many companies may think that Facebook users are predominantly young, but the data on American Facebook users contradicts that assumption. Almost 40% are over the age of 40, with women far outnumbering men in the 50-and-over category. Growth rates are highest for the 60-and-over group. So, companies whose market is a more mature crowd should not shy away from using social media: they can reach all ages on Facebook.[2]

Continuous improvement of social and mobile presence is table stakes for competing in today's world.

Analytics and Big Data

Data is being generated at an unprecedented rate, creating massive stores of information. Analytics and big data mine these colossal and diverse sets of data to find useful patterns and insights that lead to positive business outcomes, such as efficiencies, customer experience improvement, better decision-making, and new business opportunities.

A few years ago, most companies analyzed only structured data—data that had specific formats and definitions and was typically generated from transactions, such as sales history or patterns, material purchases, and employee payroll. High storage, memory, and processing costs limited the amount of data available and the analysis that could be performed on it. Today, however, companies are increasingly paying attention to unstructured data, such as social media posts, books, annual reports, and emails, allowing them to gather insights into previously opaque matters, such as reactions to new products or to service issues, which enables them to react more effectively.

The trend to analyzing unstructured data aligns with another: the trend to analyze not only internal data but external data as well. The unstructured data that businesses examine is mostly generated outside the company.

The housing of data has also evolved in recent years. In 2010, IT departments housed most data within databases tied directly to applications such as ERP, or in data warehouses that contained data that had gone through the "Extract, Transform, and Load" process. Today, in addition to these, you will find data lakes and virtualized data. A data lake stores all data in its original, unpolished form, rather than getting it ready for analysis. Structure and form are given only when you use the data, not when the data is loaded. Thanks to open-source tools like Hadoop, the cost of storing data is lower with data lakes.

Like a data lake, data virtualization leaves data in its original form. Data virtualization also leaves data in its original location—operational databases, data warehouses, Microsoft Office files, and even data lakes. A virtualization layer and tool is installed that enables access to the original data. No replication or copying of data takes place.

On the analytics side, companies are moving beyond descriptive analytics—dashboards and reports that that tell you what happened in the past but not why—to Predictive analytics—analysis of data to model and forecast future outcomes—and prescriptive analytics—making recommendations based on optimization and simulation algorithms.

Descriptive analytics are used to generate most of the reports that companies use to understand what is going on, particularly with company financials, including income statements, balance sheets, inventory movement, and customer satisfaction.

Predictive analytics are used to gain an understanding of the future and provide insights that can spur action. The data from sensors in assets predict a failure of a part, allowing for pre-emptive repair; credit scores predict the likelihood of a customer paying their bill; predictive algorithms recommend books that you are likely to enjoy; and analyzing personnel data forecasts the probability of a recruiting candidate succeeding in a new job.

Prescriptive analytics provide advice and recommendations by modeling the probable outcomes of alternative decisions. As examples, they indicate where and to what extent oil companies should drill; they give price recommendations that maximize contribution; and they prescribe the most efficient routes for deliveries.

Cloud Computing

The term "cloud" originated from the diagrams that many of us used to draw that depicted things going into and out of the Internet (and before the Internet, any network). The Internet was typically drawn as a cloud because that was an easy way to depict it. Over time, "cloud" came to be a synonym for "on the Internet," so "cloud computing" means computing on the Internet, that is, using servers and applications on the Internet rather than on company premises.

The National Institute of Standards and Technology (NIST) has an official and more precise definition of cloud computing:

"Cloud computing is a model for enabling ubiquitous, convenient, on-demand network access to a shared pool of configurable computing resources (e.g., networks, servers, storage, applications, and services) that can be rapidly provisioned and released with minimal management effort or service provider interaction."[3]

Note that by "shared pool," they mean several organizations using the same system, also known as "multi-tenant." Occasionally, software vendors claim that their software is cloud-based when they are only hosting your instance of the software. If the software is not shared with other clients, it is not technically cloud-based because it is not multi-tenant.

NIST goes on to specify alternative service models, all of which have become standard vocabulary:

Software as a Service (SaaS) is providing software that runs in the cloud. People often ask, "Is cloud the same as SaaS?" Well, SaaS is one of the three cloud service models. With SaaS, you are simply using the application and are not involved in building it, hosting it, or maintaining it. Typically, all clients use the same instance of the software, although there are usually opportunities to configure it and modify settings to your needs. The provider issues updates to the software behind the scenes. Examples of SaaS include *Salesforce.com*, Google Apps, Workday, and QuickBooks Online.

Platform as a Service (PaaS) is the provision of cloud-based tools such as programming languages used to develop and run the cloud-based software. The tools make application development, deployment, and management of the software faster and easier. You build the application and upload it to the provider's platform, where they look after performance management, security, and upgrades. You pay for the amount you use. Examples of PaaS offerings include *Force.com* or Heroku from *Salesforce.com*, Azure from Microsoft, Google App Engine, and Amazon Web Services Elastic Beanstalk.

Infrastructure as a Service (IaaS) is the provision of hardware such as computing, storage, and networking upon which the company can load and run the software. The buyer determines what they want to do with the infrastructure, so the user may decide what operating system to use and may load their own applications and data. Examples of providers of IaaS are Amazon Web Services, Azure, Rackspace, and IBM SmartCloud Enterprise.

NIST also provides useful definitions of alternative deployment models: A *private cloud* serves a single organization; a *community cloud* serves a particular set of users or organizations; a *public cloud* is used by any customer from the general public, and a *hybrid cloud* combines two or more of the above deployment models. Hybrid cloud is becoming the most common approach. Many companies use several public clouds and private clouds. RightScale Inc.'s 2016 State of the cloud study surveyed 1,060 companies and found that 95% were using cloud computing and that 71% of these were using a hybrid model.

Pros and Cons of Cloud

Cloud computing provides benefits that drive business agility, such as easier infrastructure setup, greater scalability, and improved reliability. However, many companies are discovering that an ongoing monthly or annual subscription fee can cost more in the long run than on-premise applications and infrastructure. This fact is in keeping with most things in business: leasing a building over the long run is more expensive than owning it, and "renting" people in the form of consultants for an extended period is more expensive than using employees.

Despite these drawbacks, most companies also realize that the benefit of agility outweighs the higher long-term cost of the cloud. Market opportunities come and go faster than ever before, and businesses need the agility to react and exploit those opportunities before their competitors do.

CONCLUSION

Third Digital technologies build on the Second Digital SMAC technologies, while also delivering something entirely new and unprecedented. In the next chapter, we will look at key emergent technologies from Third Digital.

Four

Key Technologies—
Third Digital

While momentum for Third Digital has been building for years, extensive use of more advanced technologies is now accelerating. Companies are beginning to embed digital technologies into their products to make them smarter and more connected, and they are significantly lowering their costs by automating their operations with cutting edge tools.

Five key technologies will drive Third Digital:

- Internet of Things (IoT)
- Machine Learning
- Natural Language Processing (NLP)
- Computer Vision
- Robotics

Interestingly, these technologies emulate certain human capabilities: learning, hearing, seeing, touching, moving. Added to the SMAC technologies described in Chapter 3, these technologies will dramatically change the way work gets done—automating physical and clerical processes and reducing costs; they will also improve the products that companies can offer, thereby making them smarter and more connected.

Of course, many other technologies are emerging for business use—for example, 3D printing, drones, the blockchain, nanobots, and wearables. I focus on the five above because these are the ones that have advanced the most in real world applications today and they are the five that I believe will have the largest impact on companies' revenue, profitability, and valuations.

How long will Third Digital last? It is impossible to tell, but one thing that seems clear is that digital transformation is accelerating. Third Digital is likely to be shorter than the 15 years of Second Digital, which itself was much shorter than the 45 years of First Digital.

The pre-digital era was the Industrial Revolution, which was a physical transformation. The mechanical and organizational improvements to efficiency it ushered in, during the late eighteenth century and through the nineteenth century, transformed agrarian and rural societies into industrial and urban ones. Technologies and developments like machinery, highways, railroads, and the steam engine physically changed the workplace and the landscape of North America and Europe.

The first and second digital eras digitized numeric and transaction-intensive processes and connected the world's population and organizations through the Internet. This digital world and the physical world remained mostly separate though. You can touch physical objects like conveyor belts, trucks, earth-moving equipment, and HVAC equipment, and most of these do not contain significant digital intelligence. Digital, on the other hand, is entirely invisible, housed away in computers and data centers. The digital tools that people and companies used in Second Digital were mostly digital-only (no physical aspects): social media, email, spreadsheets, documents, manufacturing systems, HR systems, and accounting systems serve as excellent examples.

The new era merges the physical and digital. Smart robots will move things around; parts and equipment will use sensors and sophisticated computing to see and hear and make decisions; consumer products will contain sensors; computer cameras will check for product defects and measure shopper traffic in stores.

Let's examine each of the Third Digital technologies.

INTERNET OF THINGS

There are currently over six billion devices connected to the Internet, comprising the internet of things. These devices share data with each other and with people. Forecasts vary, but we will likely see 20 to 30 billion devices on IoT by 2020, with a corresponding estimated $3–$4 trillion in global IoT spending. Industrial companies are going hard after that revenue.

The "things" part of IoT includes a wide variety of devices embedded into automobiles, motors, HVAC units, jet engines, home thermostats, power lines, and any other physical asset. It includes things on—or even inside—people, such as heart implants, fitness devices like the Fitbit, and other wearable devices. It also includes devices on animals, such as chips in farm animals or pets.

IoT Key Enabling Technologies

IoT starts with a sensor—a small electronic device installed in the asset that monitors it, collects data about it, and sends the data along. The sensor can gather such information as temperature, moisture, pressure, motion, noise, and light. Sensors are part of a category of products called MEMS, or micro-electromechanical systems, that combine computers with small mechanical devices like sensors, gears, valves, switches, and pumps.

IoT sensors include gyroscopes and accelerometers, which measure speed, direction, and acceleration; motion detectors; force gauges; microphones; moisture sensors; light sensors; thermometers; and biosensors that assess biological processes in living beings. Many of these sensors have been around for quite some time; what has changed is that their cost and size have dropped rapidly, while their processing capabilities and durability have improved. Their increased performance and convenience is what enabled the rise of the internet of things.

Many of the things connected to IoT also have actuators that convert energy to motion. Whereas sensors *send* data, actuators *receive* data and can take action based on that input. Examples of such actions include flipping on a switch; modifying the temperature, force, position of an object; turning on a water pump once the water has raised to a certain level; and sending an audible signal to a driver whose car is veering outside its lane.

IoT takes advantage of several communication technologies. RFID (radio frequency identification system) allows devices to transfer information to one another using tags attached to the assets and radio transmitters–receivers to read or send signals to the tag. RFID is commonly used to collect road tolls, access buildings, and track inventory. Near Field Communication or NFC, is another communication format that is used for devices that are very close to each other (fewer than 10 cm). For wider ranges, IoT is enabled by standard local Internet areas and wide area communications, such as WiFi, landline, and cell phone networks.

Each device uses an IP (Internet Protocol) address, the unique string of numbers separated by periods that identifies computers and other devices on the Internet. There are currently two versions of IP addresses: IPv4 and IPv6. IPv4 uses a 32-bit address, which means it allows 2^{32}, or approximately four billion (4×10^9), addresses. Clearly, with six billion devices on IoT, this is insufficient. IPv6 uses 128-bit addresses, providing 2^{128} possible unique addresses, which equals 34×10^{37}, or 340 trillion trillion trillion addresses. Thanks to IPv6, the sun is likely to burn out before we run out of IP addresses.

IoT Business Uses

IoT, along with Third Digital itself, is in its infancy, so there is no telling what kind of novel and innovative uses it will be put to as it evolves. For the moment, companies use it primarily to improve efficiency and effectiveness. Let's look at a few examples.

Asset Efficiency and Effectiveness

Sensors and transducers are being installed in most significant assets today to monitor and improve performance. Jet engines, for example, produce over 500 GB of data every flight. Sensors transmit data on the condition and performance of the engine so that short-term performance adjustments can be made and the data can be further analyzed to guide longer-term design changes that improve performance and reliability. It is the same with motors, tractors, conveyors, elevators, and most assets that are expensive and perform tasks.

IoT also drives efficiency and effectiveness by reducing the frequency of use of assets or material so that they are deployed only when needed. For example, the agricultural equipment manufacturer John Deere provides sensors that monitor the moisture in the ground, allowing irrigation equipment to be used only where and when it is required. Startup companies have developed robotic machines that are small enough to fit between rows of corn, test the soil, and dispense an optimal amount of fertilizer in targeted locations. Besides saving costs, this approach is more environmentally friendly since farmers can distribute smaller amounts of fertilizer than it would take to blanket a field.

Customer Outcomes

The efficiency and effectiveness enabled by IoT also allow companies to improve customer outcomes. Installing sensors into products and analyzing the data from the sensors is part of an overall trend to look beyond the number of goods shipped to the quality of the customers' experience once the product is delivered to them.

Heavy equipment dealers install sensors in mining and construction equipment. The sensors reduce interruptions for customers using the products by predicting when maintenance is required. They also can perform more advanced tasks like identifying the optimal and most fuel-efficient speed for a large truck given the density of the earth it is driving on.

Companies are starting to use IoT to improve customer experience and outcomes in areas other than asset management. Disneyland provides guests with wristbands that include an RFID sensor. These deliver real-time information about traffic patterns and flow, allowing the amusement park managers to understand better where bottlenecks occur and how to prevent them. Constant feedback from the wristbands improves customer experience by enabling guests to avoid waiting in long lines for attractions.

Product as a Service

IoT enables companies to move beyond selling and servicing products to offering the entire bundle of product, customer service, and customer success. An example is Car2Go, a subsidiary of Daimler. Car2Go provides cars on demand: you can pick up a car near your location and drop it off near your destination. The service would not be possible without the IoT sensors that monitor and provide condition, location, and safety information.

ARTIFICIAL INTELLIGENCE

The next three technologies we investigate—machine learning, NLP, machine vision—are areas within the overall field of artificial intelligence (AI), referring to a computer's ability to do things that normally require human intelligence. Therefore, before going into each of these three, let's examine the broader field of AI.

Researchers have pursued artificial intelligence since the beginning of the digital era, and it is only now becoming useful in a big way because of several contributing factors. First, AI requires a lot of computer processing power. The speed and volume of processing have risen dramatically in recent years, while the cost has dropped precipitously. Second, developing intelligence requires examining, parsing, and analyzing vast amounts of data. With the development of analytics and big data in Second Digital, we now have the capacity to analyze this massive data. Finally, the move to the cloud enables us to deploy far greater processing and storage.

AI is behind some of our everyday interactions with technology. Banks use it to detect charges outside of the norm to alert them to possible cases of fraud. Traders use it. You use it, perhaps unknowingly, to filter out spam emails. Web pages that help you with customer service and online help also use it. Amazon uses it to recommend books to you. It is now even used to write articles, perform medical diagnoses, and make financial planning recommendations.

MACHINE LEARNING

We are now enabling computer systems to learn. They do so by being fed mountains of information and being instructed to parse and analyze the data to identify patterns, questions, and answers. This is machine learning, and perhaps the best-known example of it is IBM's Watson.

In 2006, ten years after their Deep Blue computer defeated the chess grandmaster Garry Kasparov, IBM decided to take on a very public and high-risk challenge: build a computer system that could compete with humans on the popular trivia gameshow Jeopardy, and possibly even win against the best Jeopardy players.

Without machine learning, an approach would be for people to create a giant list of potential questions and answers. Clearly, that is not feasible. There is an infinite number of questions. Instead, IBM fed Watson data and set it up to learn. The team fed Watson over 200 million pages of text and images from dictionaries, fiction and non-fiction books, newspapers, and Web pages, including the full text of Wikipedia. They also fed it every question that Jeopardy had previously asked and their answers.

The team programmed Watson to analyze the data, build indices, and assess patterns. They developed a system whereby Watson would react to Jeopardy clues by forming hypotheses about the possible answer and then determining the probability that each answer is correct. It would then supply the answer with the highest probability of being correct.

In February 2011, Watson competed with the best players in the history of Jeopardy: Brad Rutter and Ken Jennings. The two had had previously earned more than $5 million in combined Jeopardy winnings. While there were some hiccups, like Watson repeating an answer that had been previously given by one of the human contestants (since Watson was not aware of the competitors' answers) and betting precisely calculated amounts like $6,436, rather than the round numbers typical on the show, Watson won the matches.

IBM has since commercialized Watson. Current uses include the following:[1]

- Macy's is testing "Macy's On-Call," a mobile service that allows shoppers to ask about products and services in natural English or Spanish. The company that provides the technology is Satisfy, which accesses the cloud version of Watson.
- The American Cancer Society, using data from *Cancer.org*, created a virtual advisor to enable patients to receive personalized information and advice.
- The Cleveland Clinic uses Watson to research and identify the best treatment based on a patient's cancer type and their DNA—research that is too time-consuming to be done effectively by doctors.
- The Memorial Sloan Kettering Cancer Center, the University of Texas MD Anderson Cancer Center, and the Mayo Clinic are using it to speed up DNA analysis and support doctors in making diagnoses and interpreting MRIs and X-rays.
- Under Armour created an app that acts as a personal trainer, providing users with health and fitness recommendations based on Watson's analytical insights.
- Banks such as Australia's ANZ Global Wealth and Singapore's DBS bank use it to answer customer questions and provide financial advice.
- Several organizations are using it to provide legal answers.

Investigating how Watson works provides insight into machine learning. On their website, IBM provides a video that describes the inner workings of Watson.[2] When entering a new field—like when Watson is first applied to the field of Cancer—Watson begins by learning the language and jargon. Human experts feed Watson a body of knowledge by loading relevant literature. Next, Watson pre-processes the data by building indices and other "data about the data," or metadata, that enable it to work with the content more efficiently. Then, a human trains Watson to interpret the information by uploading question and answer pairs to familiarize Watson with linguistic patterns and meaning. Watson is then ready to provide answers, recommendations, and insights. When asked questions, it creates hypotheses and searches for evidence to support them. Watson continues to learn from its interactions with users and receives new information as it is published.

Google Translate is another case of machine learning. The program learns by examining millions of pages of already translated text. Since Google launched the product in 2006, it has grown to support 103 languages and continues to learn. In April 2016, Google reported that 3.5 million people made 90 million contributions to the program through Translate Community.[3]

What makes machine learning so different is that computers no longer have to rely on humans to specify a decision tree. Rather than being told "If symptoms X appear, then the diagnosis should be Y," computers can now review the big data on symptoms and diagnoses independently and draw their own conclusions, patterns, and inferences.

I recently asked a prominent doctor if she thought computers could make a diagnosis as well or better than doctors. Probably not, she told me, because it would be doctors who inform the computer what to look for and what to conclude in the first place. If this were the approach used to train computers to diagnose, I would agree with her: you can never become better than your teachers. What she described is hand-coding a diagnostics decision tree into a computer. That is not machine learning. Machine learning is feeding the computer tons of content, and letting the computer dissect that data and look for patterns.

Why is this technology so important to businesses? It enables new products and services and it can improve customer outcomes. Furthermore, the primary role of managers is to make decisions. Machine learning can trawl through the large amounts of data that a company already has access to and help make better decisions in areas such as the following:

- Sales and Marketing: optimize promotions and rebates; personalize recommendations; sentiment analysis; pricing; customer relationship management
- Human Resources: candidate selection; staffing levels; attrition prediction
- Finance: assessing customer credit risks; trading; liquidity assessments
- Manufacturing: demand forecasting; predictive maintenance; inventory planning; optimize production workflows; optimize supply chains
- Security: identify malware; fraud detection, detect attacks and risky behavior, detect threats

NATURAL LANGUAGE PROCESSING

Natural language processing (NLP) is the ability of computers to understand human language, written or vocalized. This field of AI enables computers to capture meaning from unstructured text. NLP systems use machine learning concepts to learn languages through experience, the way humans do. Speech recognition technology complements NLP by taking voice as input and identifying the words and sentences spoken, which NLP can then interpret.

NLP and speech recognition have advanced over recent years to the point where they are now useful. They enable humans to provide instructions in natural language. Think of Apple's Siri and Amazon's Echo: we simply ask the devices to do things by using our voices and ordinary language. Airbnb uses NLP to understand and analyze written reviews and interactions between users, bypassing the need for humans to read through every single piece of text.

Almost all of a typical company's data is now digital, but only about 20% of it is structured. The rest consists of documents, emails, catalogs, reports, speeches, and videos. Also, most external data, such as social media posts, news reports, and competitor posts, are unstructured. With the ability to analyze this vast amount of information written in natural language, computers can now perform sentiment analysis, which examines social media posts and determines whether what people are saying about a company's brand and products is positive, neutral, or negative. NLP not only allows us to analyze unstructured data but can also create it. Companies such as Narrative Science offer software that can take data and turn it into understandable information. News organizations have exploited these developments and are currently using NLP to write short news articles. Chances are good that the corporate earnings report you recently read on *Forbes* or the sports story you read on AP was written by a robot.[4]

COMPUTER VISION

A related technological development is Computer Vision, which is the ability of computers to simulate human vision by capturing and understanding digital images and videos. The term "machine vision" refers to roughly the same process but in a more narrow, industrial context. Computer Vision took a leap forward in 2010 when Microsoft released their Kinect video game console, which allowed gamers to play Xbox games without interacting with any of the Xbox hardware's physical interface. Kinect included a digital camera, a depth sensor, and a microphone, all of which enabled 3D motion capture and facial recognition. What was revolutionary about this technology was that it was available for the relatively affordable price of $150. Within weeks, researchers and hackers, recognizing its potential, had reverse engineered it to understand the technology and leverage it in other products.[5]

Computer Vision is the technology that Facebook employs to recognize and identify people in photographs and that your smartphone camera uses when it puts a square around the faces of individuals you are shooting. If you drive a late model car, it probably alerts you when you try to make a lane change and there is another vehicle in your blind spot—another example of computer vision in action.

Businesses put Computer Vision to a variety of uses. One of its primary purposes is to enable the robotics that we will describe in the next section. There are also many non-robotic uses: systems that watch products on factory lines to identify defects; autonomous vehicles that read speed limits and other signs; airport security scanners that recognize your face and pull up any data associated with it; and in-store systems that help retailers track shopper traffic through the store and determine the demographics of the shoppers.

ROBOTICS

Second Digital technologies, especially cloud and big data, and the technologies described above, all combine to create the condition for robotics to flourish and for companies to take advantage of the automation and efficiency improvements that robotics enable. We are on the cusp of North American industry regaining a substantial competitive advantage in both the manufacturing and service sectors by automating work.

The intelligence, seeing, and hearing described above enable advanced robots to do tasks that were unheard of just a few years ago. In agriculture, for example, robots can now serve as expert fruit pickers, able to recognize the degree of ripeness of strawberries and gently pick only those ready for consumption. Robots can identify and remove unwanted weeds while leaving surrounding plants untouched. Their capabilities are so advanced that the Japanese company Spread has a farm run entirely by robots, which harvest 30,000 heads of lettuce every day.

Robots have been employed in factories for a while now but, until recently, they simply weren't very smart. And without vision, they relied on consistent position and timing to perform tasks. When it came to picking products in warehouses, packing them into boxes, and loading them into trucks, humans, with the benefit of sensory experience, were by far better equipped. Without sensors or artificial intelligence, robots were unable to recognize individual boxes, pick them up without damaging them, and infer ways to load them onto the truck. All that has changed. Adidas even has a plant in Germany that is almost entirely automated. They do have ten employees, but they expect to reduce the already small headcount in the near future.

The hospitality industry employs robots to prepare meals and drinks and to deliver room service. Guests on Royal Caribbean's Anthem of the Seas ship can enjoy cocktails made for them by robots developed at MIT. Starwood's robot, the aptly named Botlr, delivers items to rooms; Hilton is testing Connie, a robot that uses the Watson AI; and WayBlazer's travel recommendation engine provides concierge advice to guests seeking tourist attractions, dining suggestions, and hotel amenities.

Robotics have resulted in significant gains for retail and e-commerce companies. Quiet Logistics, an e-commerce fulfillment center, expects to increase productivity 800% by using robots to fetch orders and bring them to warehouse employees. Five-foot tall robots in certain Lowes stores speak five languages, use Computer Vision recognition software to recognize humans, ask what you are looking for, and then instruct you to follow them to the item.[6]

Most of the examples discussed so far are of robots performing tasks that require movement, but there is another field that uses robotics to automate back office processes. Robotic process automation, also known as Intelligent Automation, uses software robots that learn to perform tasks that were previously done by humans. Processes that are rule-based and involve data entry and data validation are good candidates for this, including:

- Data verification (e.g., verifying that payroll data matches ERP data)
- Underwriting insurance applications
- Evaluating credit card applications
- Answering invoice queries
- Processing sales orders, including checking the order data, checking inventory, and allocating the order to specific warehouses
- Assessing the feasibility of meter reading
- Data updates (e.g., changes of address)

Using RPA is like having a virtual employee who processes work using existing systems. Thanks to machine learning, RPA can learn as it works rather than relying on someone attempting to program the system with all the rules ahead of time. Moreover, software robots are not only more efficient than humans, but they are also less prone to errors.

We know that, to some extent, robots—whether mechanical or software—will replace human workers. However, we also know that they will provide support to the people who do remain part of the workforce. They will enable us to perform our jobs better by applying their learning abilities, extensive computational capability, and ready access to big data.

Consider a lung cancer specialist interpreting an MRI. The specialist has treated lung cancer patients for many years and has a hypothesis about the most appropriate treatments. There is, however, no way for one specialist to keep up with all the new research and treatments discussed in technical journals. She may want to ask deeper questions to see what other experts have experienced when treating the same type of lung cancer. She may want to ask for evidence and conduct a dialog with the cognitive system to understand context and relationships. With advanced robotics at her disposal, she could get those answers instead of making decisions without the benefit of more extensive information.

KPMG uses Watson to support their audit and tax staff. The computer can analyze large volumes of structured and unstructured data related to a company's financial information, while auditors "teach" the technology how to fine-tune its assessments over time. This approach gives audit teams faster access to increasingly precise measurements that help them analyze anomalies and assess whether additional steps should be taken.[7]

Cognitive technology allows a larger percentage of the data to be analyzed, giving KPMG professionals the potential to obtain enhanced insights into a client's financial and business operations. At the same time, cognitive-enabled processes allow auditors to focus on higher value activities, including offering additional insights concerning risks and other related findings.

IMPACT ON EMPLOYMENT

Third Digital will enable companies to do more work with fewer employees. Technologies introduced in this era have already had a significant societal impact and sparked a large debate. Some people believe that robotic process automation is good. It will enable us to move to less menial jobs that are more suitable to us—jobs that require creativity and human interaction. It is also possible that the enormous wave of automation that is about to occur will enable North America to reverse the offshoring trend and bring more manufacturing back to the continent. And even though most work will be automated, humans will still be needed to support the automated production.

Others believe that a significant portion of today's jobs is at risk of disappearing without much opportunity for replacement. A study by Oxford University and MIT bears out this fear, indicating that 47% of jobs are at high risk of being eliminated.[8]

I believe this is an issue we need to take seriously. Full employment may not be required to produce the goods and services that we wish to consume. Companies need to make use of the automation opportunities or risk going out of business. Retraining displaced workers to perform new jobs is only feasible to a certain extent, so there is a risk of higher unemployment. As business leaders, we are heading the social transformations brought on by our use of Third Digital technologies. We have, then, a responsibility to lend our voices to these debates and to participate in the search for solutions.

CONCLUSION

These four chapters conclude Part 1, which focused on information about the emerging digital world. Part 2 shifts to action—establishing a vision and leveraging digital to improve products, processes, and the customer journey.

How to Thrive in Digital

Part Two is about how to excel in the digital world. Chapter 5 describes steps to creating a company vision for applying digital technology. Chapters 6, 7, and 8 outline leading practices for building digital into products, processes, and the customer journey, respectively. Finally, Chapter 9 sets out tools to help you take action on your company's digital vision.

The business literature is active with books, papers, and blog posts about digital transformation, what it is, and how to achieve it. Frequently, they contain anecdotes about what certain companies are doing to adapt to new digital realities. This chapter provides some stories but also strives to present a more holistic view of how to leverage digital developments in processes found throughout the entire company.

For a comprehensive set of business processes, we use the APQC Process Classification Framework (PCF). APQC (American Productivity and Quality Center) is a member-based, non-profit organization, and is the leading authority on benchmarking, best practices, process and performance improvement, and knowledge management.[1] According to the APQC, their "Process Classification Framework® (PCF) is the most used process framework in the world. It creates a common language for organizations to communicate and define work processes comprehensively and without redundancies."[2]

The Process Classification Framework is a taxonomy of business processes, organized into thirteen Level 1 processes. For this book, I combine "Deliver Physical Products" and "Deliver Services" into one process, "Deliver Physical Products and Services," because the digital best practices are similar for both. So, we examine practices for the twelve Level 1 processes show below. (They are not in the same order as the official APQC framework; the order used is more conducive to the structure of this book.)

Chapter 5, "Setting Your Digital Vision", covers the following APQC process:

- Develop Vision and Strategy

Chapter 6, "Adding Digital to Products", covers the following processes:

- Develop and Manage Products and Services

Chapter 7, "Digitizing Processes" covers the following:

- Deliver Physical Products and Services
- Develop and Manage Human Capital
- Manage Information Technology (IT)
- Manage Financial Resources
- Acquire, Construct, and Manage Assets
- Manage Enterprise Risk, Compliance, Remediation, and Resiliency
- Manage External Relationships
- Develop and Manage Business Capabilities

Chapter 8, "Improving the Customer Journey", covers the following:

- Market and Sell Products and Services
- Manage Customer Service

Throughout Part 2, I present a small number of examples of leading digital practices for each process. The examples are meant to stimulate your thinking, not to serve as a comprehensive list. For people who like more detail, you can download a more complete list on our website *www.thirddigital.com.*

Five

Setting Your Digital Vision

How your company navigates the digital world, which technologies it deploys, and what outcomes it wishes to generate should all be driven by a digital vision (Figure 5-1). A vision identifies what the company will reach for—a description of where it wants to go. The digital vision states how the company will leverage digital technologies to improve products, processes, and the customer journey. In this chapter, we describe these three areas in more detail, discuss an approach to prioritizing, and suggest a high-level framework for the digital vision.

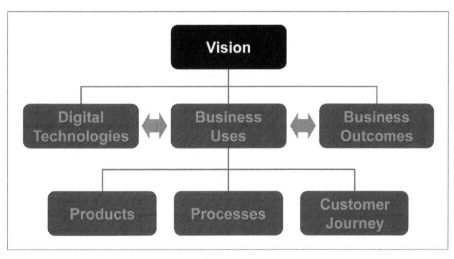

Figure 5-1: Vision

PRODUCTS, PROCESSES, CUSTOMER JOURNEY

For this book, "product" means *what* the company provides and what its customers pay for and receive. (And recall from Chapter 1 that we use "product" in the generic sense to refer to both tangible products and services.) For example, General Motors' product is vehicles; a hospital's product is health care; Walmart and Amazon's product is merchandise. "Process" is *how* the company provides the product. For example, a company's process may include designing, manufacturing, and selling the product. It would also include managing human resources and finance. "Customer journey" refers to the steps and actions the customer undertakes to find the product, order it, pay for it, receive it, and use it.

To illustrate, consider the products, processes, and journey for ten well-known companies listed in Table 5-1. (Of course, the products and processes are rather over-simplified in the table.)

Company	Products	Process	Customer Journey
McDonald's	Food	Prepare and provide fast meals in company stores	Get to the store, order, and pay
Google	Audience	Deliver an audience through a search engine	Create ad, select keywords, run ad, monitor
Facebook	Audience	Deliver an audience through a social network	Create ad, select audience, run ad, monitor
Amazon (Retail)	500 million products	Provide products through e-commerce	Search products online, order, pay, receive at home
Walmart	5 million products	Provide products through retail outlets	Get to the store, pick products, pay, return home
Alibaba	1 billion products	Provide platform for connecting buyers and sellers	Search products online, order, pay, receive at home
Uber	Rides	Provide a platform for connecting drivers and riders. Recognize rider location, match to the closest driver, process payment	Order ride, rate the driver
GM	Vehicles	Create, manufacture, sell through dealers	Research online, visit dealers, test drive, haggle, pay
Apple	Digital devices	Design, manufacture, sell direct	Order online or at stores, select, pay

Table 5-1. Product, Process, and Journey Examples

Now, some companies are more known for one of the three areas than the others. Apple is known for its well-designed and easily usable products; Walmart's processes are world-class in their efficiency; Amazon's customers rave about the ease of shopping and fast delivery—the customer journey.

An excellent process can form the basis for providing other products. Amazon started as a bookstore, but their effective process enabled them to add other merchandise. Their process also allowed them to provide Amazon Web Services' on-demand cloud computing services. Uber started as a ride-sharing service, but their process could then be used to provide food delivery.

So how does this relate to setting a digital vision? When it comes to products, companies are looking to maximize value; for process, minimize cost and effort; for customer journey, make it as easy as possible to get the product and to achieve the desired customer outcome. The vision supports these objectives. Also, the uses of digital technology are different for each of the three areas. For products, companies will *provide* digital by embedding it into products or by providing digital-only products, such as apps or information. For processes, companies *use* digital technology to automate, speed up, and improve the reliability of processes, all at a lower cost. To improve the customer journey, companies will both use and provide digital technology.

FRAMEWORK FOR A DIGITAL VISION

A vision is not a lengthy document—just a few sentences. It should address questions across the three areas as presented in Table 5-2.

Products—Maximize the value	Processes—Minimize the cost and effort	Customer Journey—Minimize the cost and effort
What digital technology or information is valuable to customers and should be embedded into our products or provided as a service?	How do we minimize movement and automate processes and make them faster, more reliable, and lower cost?	How can digital make the customer processes, such as ordering, receiving, getting service, and using the products easier?

Table 5-2. Digital Vision Questions

The digital vision must support the company's business strategy and activate your overall company vision, mission, and purpose. Further, it should be aligned with today's customers and the expected customer desires three to five years out.

Looking at a few examples is useful. Of course, companies do not publish their digital vision, but we can look in the annual reports to see examples of what companies wish to achieve and are reaching for with respect to leveraging digital technologies to improve products, processes, and the customer journey. Following are several examples.

Bank of Montreal
Excerpts from the 2015 Annual Report related to digital vision:

"A more personal bank for a digital world. Smart branches where digital and human interactions blend seamlessly. ABMs with video tellers offering immediate expert help. Ideas tailored to customers' needs using data-driven insights. Fast, secure mobile payments, and cash withdrawals using only a smartphone. A tablet app that integrates personal banking with investing and financial management. A callback feature that actually calls you back. And access to all of our products and services through single points of contact. This is what "we are here to help" means in the digital age. We make banking easier. Smarter. And flexible enough to fit comfortably into our customers' busy, connected lives."

"… simplifying and automating for greater efficiency. Focus on efficiency through technology innovation, simplifying and automating processes, and extending the digital experience across our channels."

Let's parse the Bank of Montreal example into the three questions that comprise a digital vision (Table 5-3):

Products—Maximize the value	Processes—Minimize the cost and effort	Customer Journey—Minimize the cost and effort
- Smart branches where digital and human interactions blend seamlessly - ABMs with video tellers offering immediate expert help - Fast, secure mobile payments - A tablet app that integrates personal banking with investing and financial management	- Ideas tailored to customers' needs using data-driven insights - Efficiency through technology innovation, simplifying, and automating processes	- Cash withdrawals using only a smartphone - Access to all of our products and services through single points of contact - Banking flexible enough to fit comfortably into our customers' busy, connected lives

Table 5-3. Bank of Montreal Digital Vision Example

Interestingly, their products are so focused on the customer journey that some of the items listed under Products could be listed under Customer Journey and vice-versa. Also, many of their statements are great examples of fusing physical and digital:

- Digital and human interactions blend seamlessly
- ABMs (physical) with video tellers (physical and digital) offering immediate expert help
- Smart (digital) branches (physical)
- Cash withdrawals (physical) using only a smartphone (digital)

They also provide a blend of *using* digital (efficiency through technology innovation) and *providing* digital (smartphone apps, mobile payments).

Stanley Black and Decker
Excerpts from the 2015 Annual Report related to digital vision:

"Digital Excellence is a comprehensive initiative designed to leverage the power of digital technology and advanced analytics to challenge existing paradigms and improve our products, processes, business models, and how our people operate. We are infusing new talent and capabilities into our organization and promoting the concepts of digital speed and leadership agility to keep our culture and enterprise fresh and relevant in this era of constantly accelerating change. Digital, including social, mobile, internet of things and big data, touches all aspects of our business and contributes to growth, margin expansion, and asset efficiency.

"... developing breakthrough innovation culture to identify and bring to market disruptive products."

"... become more effective and efficient in our customer-facing processes resulting in continued share gains and margin expansion throughout our businesses."

Again, let's parse the above (Table 5-4):

Products—Maximize the value	Processes—Minimize the cost and effort	Customer Journey—Minimize the cost and effort
- Leverage digital technology to improve our products - Bring to market disruptive products - Breakthrough innovation	- Leverage digital technology to improve our processes - Digital speed	- Become more effective and efficient in our customer-facing processes

Table 5-4. Stanley Black and Decker Digital Vision Example

Note that the three areas—product, process, customer journey—do not need to have equal weight in the vision. In fact, in many cases, they should not; companies need to focus. Stanley Black and Decker's 2015 annual report spends significant time outlining how they are improving products and setting up the company culture and processes to support product improvements. Not much time is spent talking about improving the customer journey. There is probably a good reason for this. They are very much a product-centric company. They sell through retailers.

Success for a company like this is dependent on having better products than competitors, so that is where the effort is.

NIKE

Excerpts from the 2015 Annual Report related to digital vision:

"Long-term growth is about more than what we make—it's how we bring it to life in the marketplace."

"Our consumers live in a digital world, and we are focused on giving them what they want: easier access to product, more real-time feedback on their performance, and a unified community for continued inspiration. Deeply personal and responsive, our digital ecosystem drives strong relationships, growing the NIKE+ community exponentially every year. We are committed to driving growth by engaging all athletes, through online, in-store, and live experiences."

"… we invest in integrating digital and physical retail seamlessly, giving our consumers better access to the products they want. And it is why we work closely with our best wholesale partners to transform the consumer experience."

"We know when consumers shop online they want a seamless, personalized, premium experience—and we deliver it on NIKE.com. While we are proud of achieving the milestone of $1 billion in revenue for NIKE.com, we are only scratching the surface of what's possible with e-commerce, which remains one of the company's largest growth opportunities."

"… expand the market through the right growth accelerators: digital platforms, advanced manufacturing, supply chain innovation, and new partnerships."

"…The insights we draw from these deep connections drive our work to innovate new products and services that engage and inspire."

And now the parsing (Table 5-5):

Products—Maximize the value	Processes—Minimize the cost and effort	Customer Journey—Minimize the cost and effort
- Innovate new products	- Advanced manufacturing - Supply chain innovation	- Easier access to product, more real-time feedback on their performance and a unified community for continued inspiration - Engaging all athletes, through online, in-store and live experiences - Transform the consumer experience - Seamless, personalized, premium experience—and we deliver it on NIKE.com. - Integrate digital and physical retail seamlessly

Table 5-5. Nike Digital Vision Example

Once again, an example of prioritizing. In their 2015 annual report, while Nike certainly points out their leading and innovative products, and improving processes, they spend more time discussing what they are doing to improve the customer journey, and in fact, the entire customer experience. An athletic shoe and apparel company would not succeed if their products were great but their customer experience was inferior.

Pitney Bowes

Excerpts from the 2015 Annual Report related to digital vision:

"That's us. Trusted craftsmen who help 1.5 million small businesses and 90% of the Fortune 500 power their commerce across the physical and digital landscape. We're one of the only companies who can help you do business in both these worlds."

"Transformation, however, is not about building an entirely new company. It's about building on what has always made us great while also taking advantage of new opportunities and addressing the evolving needs of our clients. This means leading not only in areas where we've always excelled, but extending our leadership into new realms, delivering physical and digital solutions that enable clients to succeed today."

"Our technologies, assets, and expertise in physical and digital commerce are a significant advantage across our portfolio. They enable our mail business to leverage digital technology from our software business to create innovative products, and our software business to leverage mail business channels to sell digital products to our worldwide base."

I'll save you the parsing on this one, but it highlights two other points about the digital vision. First, fusing of digital and physical. Almost every statement quoted by Pitney Bowes above is based on that concept. Second, they say that transformation in *not* about building a new company. Indeed. Many folks in my industry (consulting) are quick to tell companies that they need to transform into a different company, create and implement new business models, or emulate the practices of fast-growing, money-losing startups. That advice is dangerous. What most companies need to do is apply digital to products, processes, and the customer journey within their existing business model, which has been successful for many years.

PRIORITIZING

The product, process, journey delineation also helps us figure out which industries are more prone to digital disruption, which, in turn, helps set a context for the vision.

There are three primary ways that companies can take market share from competitors:

- Improving the product, making it better for the customer
- Improving internal processes required to provide the product, reducing the company's expense, thereby making the product available at lower cost to the customer

- Improving customer journey, make getting and receiving the product, and achieving the desired customer outcomes, easier for them

Determining which of these areas is a higher priority over others depends on whether your product is differentiated or is more of a commodity. For purposes of this book, a differentiated product is one in which there are meaningful differences from one product to another. Examples include fashion clothing, software, buildings, restaurants, and fine art. A commodity product is one in which customers do not see much of a difference from one supplier to another. Examples include electricity, gasoline, fruits and vegetables, lumber, and basic professional services like will preparation.

With a differentiated product, the product itself is paramount. With a commodity product, price, and ease of doing business are paramount.

Figure 5-2 outlines which of the three approaches—making the product better, reducing costs by improving the processes, or making the customer journey easier—is more likely to be used to shake up an industry, depending on whether your product is differentiated or is a commodity.

	Digital Enables Product Improvements **Better**	Digital Enables Internal Process Improvements **Lower Cost**	Digital Enables Customer Process Improvements **Easier**
Differentiated Products	1. Disruption Likely	2. Disruption Possible	3. Disruption Possible
Commodity Products	4. Not Applicable	5. Disruption Likely	6. Disruption Likely

Figure 5-2: Disruption Opportunities

For *differentiated* products, if digital innovations allow someone to build a better product (Square 1), they can take market share. What matters is the product itself. Lower cost (Square 2) and ease of ordering/ receiving (Square 3) are less important, although they can still play a role.

For *commodity* products, there is, by definition, not much opportunity to improve the product (Square 4). However, if digital technology improves internal processes that leads to reduced operating costs and enables a lower price (Square 5), a disruptor can capture a larger share of the market. Similarly, if digital technology enables improvements to the customer's journey for getting the commodity product—for example selecting, ordering, and receiving the product—a disruptor can gain market share (Square 6).

So, the opportunities and threats are primarily in Squares 1, 5, and 6.

Setting a digital vision should start with an assessment of which square your company or your lines of business are in. Chances are good that you have different products in different squares. Your highest priority initiatives should be in the squares where disruption is most likely.

Second Digital Disruption Examples

It is useful to examine industries that were disrupted in Second Digital and bring those lessons into the visioning exercises for Third Digital.

Figure 5-3 shows some of the disruption that occurred during Second Digital. That era enabled a far superior differentiated product (Square 1) in the area of advertising, for example. Before search engines and social media, advertisers had no way of pinpointing potential customers or of tracking the effectiveness of their advertising campaigns. Television, radio, newspapers, magazines, and billboards were the best media available to them. In Second Digital, Google enabled advertising that is tailored and presented directly to a single person who most likely has a problem that your product can solve. Facebook enabled advertisers to reach the largest audience ever—1.5 billion people—and to target them with products aligned with their particular interests.

As another example, still in Square 1, consider consumer electronics. Apple was able to offer a substantially better designed MP3 player—the iPod—which enabled them to take over that market. Interestingly, while the device itself, the iPod, is in Square 1, the songs, provided through iTunes, are in Square 6. The player is a differentiated product, but the song files are commodities. The MP3 data file that comprises the Beach Boys song "Good Vibrations" stayed the same, whether you purchased it from Sony or Apple. So, with iTunes, Apple made it much easier (Square 6) to obtain the file and enjoy the music, in particular for users of their MP3 players. Therefore, iPod/iTunes took enormous market share in the music industry by hitting both Square 1 and Square 6.

	Digital Enables Product Improvements **Better**	Digital Enables Internal Process Improvements **Lower Cost**	Digital Enables Customer Process Improvements **Easier**
Differentiated Products	1. Disruption Likely • Advertising (Google, Facebook) • Consumer Electronics (iPod)	2. Disruption Possible	3. Disruption Possible
Commodity Products	4. Not Applicable	5. Disruption Likely • Computing (Amazon Web Services) • Publishing (Amazon Publishing) • Taxi (Uber)	6. Disruption Likely • Music Retail (iTunes) • Retail (Amazon Retail) • Taxi (Uber)

Figure 5-3: Second Digital Disruption

There are several examples of Second Digital technologies that enable internal process improvements (Square 5) and reduce costs. Amazon Web Services became a $10-billion-dollar technology company in just ten years. They were able to achieve that growth by changing the traditional process of selling on-premise computers, like HP, IBM, and Dell, to providing on-demand computing services. The customers could obtain their desired outcome—access to computing power—at a lower cost.

Amazon also lowered the cost of book publishing (Square 5) by changing that industry's processes. Authors can now self-publish their work through Kindle Direct Publishing (for eBooks). In traditional publishing, approximately 80% of the cost of a book is eaten up by printing and distribution.[1] With the introduction of the Kindle, Amazon lowered that cost to a fraction by eliminating the need to print hardcopies, bind them, and ship the printed copies to bookstores in the hope that they would sell. Now, only data needs to be sent electronically, bypassing the need to pay those fees, yielding lower costs to readers, and leaving a higher portion of the profits to Amazon and the authors.

Amazon Retail is solidly in Square 6. Amazon dramatically simplified the customer journey of selecting, ordering, and receiving merchandise. Most of the merchandise itself is the same whether you buy it from Amazon or another retailer, so it qualifies as commodity. Amazon made finding, selecting, ordering, paying, and receiving the merchandise far easier. Rather than visiting multiple stores, consumers can order from Amazon in minutes.

Uber's disruption is in both Square 5 and Square 6. In Square 5, they took the commodity of rides and implemented lower cost processes—although some would argue they also ignored laws in place that govern taxi services. To reduce company process costs (Square 5), Uber fully automated the dispatching of rides. Compare that to traditional taxi services, which have manual work involved in receiving requests for rides and communicating them to drivers. Uber also made the customer process significantly easier (Square 6). Rather than dialing a number, explaining your pickup and drop off locations to a dispatcher, and adding the tip and paying the bill at the end, the customer just needs to request a ride with a couple of clicks or taps on the Uber app.

Of course, all the Second Digital examples have the benefit of 20/20 hindsight. Predicting *future* disruption is not such a clear-eyed matter. Still, looking at recent technology-based disruptions gives us useful insights into the mechanics of disruption and possible winners. Although the technologies are different in Third Digital, the model remains the same and companies can use it to locate their threats and opportunities as background for setting their vision.

Third Digital Disruption

The winners in Third Digital will be companies that can leverage digital to substantially improve differentiated products and companies that can simplify operational processes and the customer journey for commodity products. Traditional companies should have the advantage: if they can leverage digital to make their existing products better, cheaper, and easier to get, they can be the disruptors instead of the disrupted.

Figure 5-4 shows examples of industries likely to be disrupted in Third Digital.

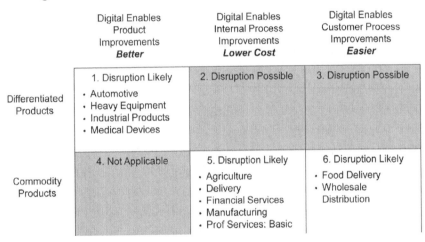

Figure 5-4: Third Digital Disruption

Square 1 Industries

Industries with differentiated products susceptible to disruption (Square 1) are those whose products can be substantially improved by being made smarter and more connected. We see this in the automotive industry, where implementing intelligence for assisted driving, navigation, entertainment, safety, and condition monitoring make a better product.

Most industrial products—machines, motors, HVAC, hydraulics, lathes—all have the opportunity for substantial improvement in Third Digital. Sensors can make these products intelligent, leading to improved uptime, reliability, and performance, along with providing ample amounts of usage and outcome data that will enable companies to make fact-based decisions about how to adjust their usage to drive better customer outcomes.

Embedded intelligence in medical devices will enable the collection of data that can be used to design and drive improvements in the products. Wearables that track conditions of the body are becoming more common and will generate substantial real-time data that can be analyzed at individual and group levels. To that data, we will also add information collected from ingestible sensors. That data can then be integrated with medical records to formulate powerful insights.

Square 5 Industries

In Square 5, industries with commodity products are prone to disruption from lower costs. First, consider agriculture. Third Digital will allow food to be produced at a substantially lower cost. CNH Industrial demonstrated a self-driving tractor at the 2016 National Farm Machinery Show. This product goes beyond the current self-steering tractors and will enable harvesting work to continue 24 hours a day—not just during daylight hours. While the tractor still needs to be monitored by humans, that monitoring could take place away from the field, and one person could watch several tractors at a time.

Products will continue to evolve to allow more precision and greater yield in agriculture, including yield monitors, variable rate machinery, soil sensors, seed-optimization applications, and precision robotic fertilizer dispensers.

Another industry ready for a shake-up is delivery. Whoever reduces the cost of last mile delivery will gain market share. "Last mile" refers to the delivery from the closest fulfillment center to the home or business. Robotics, drones, traffic data, and automated vehicles are being used in combination to reduce the delivery time and cost. Companies are also experimenting with "click and collect" processes to reduce cost further. These delivery models involve the customer picking up the item at a location at a time convenient to them. Customers have ever-escalating expectations when it comes to the speed of delivery and leveraging Third Digital technology to reduce costs will be necessary to meet those expectations.

Lower cost will also disrupt the financial services industry and basic professional services. Artificial intelligence will reduce the manual effort involved in providing financial advice and basic legal services, such as real estate transactions, wills, and accounting and bookkeeping.

The increased presence of robots in the manufacturing industry will continue to drive down costs. Companies most effective at deploying robotics will be able to offer consumers a lower price and, as a result, will gain market share.

Square 5 disruption is not providing a lower functionality product for a lower price. It is applying digital technologies to reduce the cost of the present high quality and high functionality products—there is no trade-off, only gain. Companies that are already established in these industries are best poised to be the disruptors. They already have the products and know how to provide them. All they need to do is develop the digital acumen and capability to apply digital innovations to their existing process.

Square 6 Industries

In Square 6, a few industries are naturally prone to Third Digital disruption by disruptors providing greater ease of ordering and receiving for customers. Getting meals is likely to become much easier. As companies start making use of robots, predictive ordering, autonomous delivery, and en-route preparation, consumers will be able to order and receive meals faster and more easily. Ordering out will continue to replace preparing meals at home.

Wholesale distribution and industrial sales will be disrupted by companies that can make the selection and ordering process substantially easier, in a manner similar to what Amazon did for consumers. Parts that know they need to be replaced and prepare purchase orders on their own; supply containers that know their contents are low and need to be reordered; and image recognition, where a repair person can snap a picture of a part and a draft of a purchase order for it will automatically be prepared—all of these will soon be commonplace.

EXTERNAL AND INTERNAL ASSESSMENT

Setting a digital vision requires understanding your company's position in this six-square framework and the potential threats and opportunities that this position entails. It is useful to conduct a self-assessment to identify this. While all companies need to move swiftly on digital transformation, those in the squares that are prone to disruptions have a particular urgency to address threats or exploit opportunities.

Assessing the external world means looking at what your competitors are doing digitally and which upstarts are beginning to encroach on your market. It is also important to know your competitors' digital vision. It is not public information, but you can find clues in earnings calls, annual reports, and news articles.

Some companies actively follow competitors' social media. How active are your competitors on social media, what is their fan-to-follower ratio, what type of content are they posting, and how engaged are their fans regarding responding to posts? You can line up your numbers against those of your competitors to identify which ones are outperforming you online. How have they acquired more fans and generated more engagement? Are they posting different types of content than you are? Is it more engaging? Are they doing it at a different frequency?

These types of assessments contribute to understanding the current state as a basis for your digital vision.

CONCLUSION

Your vision will define where to focus your digital initiatives: making products smarter, driving efficiencies in internal processes, improving the customer journey, or some combination of all three. The next three chapters examine how to execute in each of these three areas.

Six

Adding Digital to Products

As we saw in Chapter 5, there are three types of business uses of digital technology: improving products, streamlining processes, and improving the customer journey. This chapter focuses on deploying digital into your products (or services) (Figure 6-1).

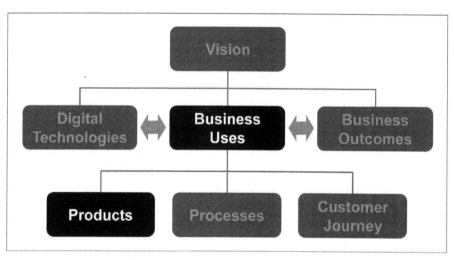

Figure 6-1: Business Uses: Products

PRODUCT PLANNING IN THIRD DIGITAL

The lifeblood of any company is new products. In Third Digital, companies generate new ideas for products by first considering how to embed digital technology into their products and services. Currently, some products and services tend to be predominantly physical, like taxi rides, furniture, and food. Some products, like software, music, and apps, are mostly digital. And others incorporate both, like Uber rides (physical movement of passengers plus digital interface, tracking, and rating); smartphones (digital technology packaged in a physical device); and modern automobiles (traditional vehicle plus navigation, sensors, and semi-autonomous driving). The largest market opportunities for the next decade will be for products and services that are both physical and digital.

A new product or service may be a new or enhanced offering in an existing market—for example, new phone models with more advanced features. Alternatively, the new offering may create a new or redefined market, as the iPhone did for the phone market. In a *Harvard Business Review* article, "Identify Blue Oceans By Mapping Your Product Portfolio," W. Chan Kim and Renee Mauborgne discuss a study that showed that 86% of new product introductions were in the Existing Markets space, while 14% were in the New or Redefined Market Space. However, only 39% of the profits came from the Existing Market space, while 61% of the profits came from the smaller set of product introductions in the New or Redefined space[1]—Something to consider when planning your evolving product portfolio.

In developing embedded-digital products, many companies are setting up innovation labs that perform discovery research; analyze the industry, competitors, and emerging technologies; and identify opportunities for new or improved products and services. The labs tend to collaborate with customers, suppliers, governments, and peer companies to innovate.

Many companies have embraced the idea of Minimal Viable Product, or MVP, that came out of the technology startup industry. This idea is a method of gauging interest by creating a product that has just enough functionality to be usable and is ready to be released to the market. There is no need to add features if the market does not value even the minimal functionality.

As a backdrop for why and how to embed digital, consider why customers purchase products in the first place. They buy products to achieve an outcome. Building managers buy heating and air conditioning equipment to provide a comfortable environment within a building. Construction site managers buy tractors to move dirt. Marketers purchase advertising to sell product. People buy tennis rackets to play tennis. Drivers buy cars to have constant access to transportation. You get the idea.

Embedding digital helps customers achieve their outcomes more effectively. The technology helps in four areas: Monitor, Analyze, Adjust, Recommend.

Once the product is put into use, it must be in good operating condition to achieve the customer's desired outcome. The better the reliability, uptime, and performance of the product, the better the outcome. Therefore, installing sensors into the product that *monitor* its condition, and thereby maximize the quality of its operations, makes sense. That is why most of the one million parts that comprise an aircraft are continuously monitored for condition and performance. Factory machines are monitored for the same reason.

Monitoring alone, though, does nothing. The real value lies in accumulating data over the cloud and *analyzing* it to make *adjustments*. Some adjustments can be done automatically. For example, the speed of a fan within an air conditioning unit may be automatically increased if the filter becomes dirty, requiring the fan to work harder to force the necessary amount of air through. Or sensors may indicate that certain plants need more fertilizer than others and automatically supply their need.

Some adjustments require the more extensive analysis of big data analytics. The analysis results in *recommendations* that are then presented for consideration. For example, some progressive tractor distributors offer a service to monitor operator gestures, fuel efficiency, and volume of earth moved, and then to analyze the data gathered, including comparing it to data for other customers and making recommendations to improve fuel and efficiency and overall tractor effectiveness by changing certain operator gestures or behaviors.

Many products must be paired with a human operator to achieve the desired outcome, like a tractor and a driver. For those products, improving customer outcomes requires assessing the operator and the product together.

Embedding digital into products is perhaps best understood by considering some examples. The ones provided below are either already being sold or are at a late stage of development. Moreover, in each case, these are products that were once 100% physical but now have a digital component.

CONSUMER EXAMPLES

Window Coverings: There are smart window blinds that automatically rise or lower based on the amount of sunlight.

Lighting: You can control smart light bulbs with an app on your phone. If you forget to turn them off when you leave the house or want to turn them on to make it look like someone is home, you do that through the app. You can even use the GPS on your phone to turn lights off automatically when you are away. You can also purchase bulbs that integrate with Amazon's Echo so you can control them with your voice.[2]

Door Locks: There are many locks available that allow entry via RFID, Bluetooth, or biometric identification (fingerprint). Bluetooth-enabled locks can sense you approaching based on your phone and unlock the door. You can also use your phone to unlock the door remotely to allow a trusted person to enter.[3]

Luggage: You can now buy a carry-on bag that you can lock and unlock with your phone or with your fingerprint, charge your devices with, locate anywhere in the world, and check its weight at any time. Companies are even working on self-propelled luggage that stays within six inches of its owner by itself. Samsonite is partnering with airlines to create a luggage bag with the ability to check itself in.[4]

Sporting Goods: Sporting goods companies have recognized that one of the outcomes their customers want is improved performance in their respective sports. They have begun to embed digital into their products to collect data that connects with smartphone or cloud apps, which then provide personalized coaching recommendations. Here are a few examples:

- Balls: Adidas makes a soccer ball that detects speed, spin, strike, and flight path and sends that data to the player's or coach's smartphone. The app can make recommendations and track the player's improvement. Wilson makes a basketball and football with similar features.[5]

- Add-on Sensors: Several companies are creating the sensor only, and not the actual sporting good. FWD Powershot offers a sensor for hockey sticks that tracks use of the stick and provides recommendations for improving play and shots. Game Golf Live provides a tag that attaches to the top of a golf club and a tracking device the player mounts on their belt to gather stats to track progress and improvements. Zepp provides a similar sensor for baseball bats. Sensors can also be attached to running shoes to measure running time, pace, distance, and stride.

- Tennis Rackets: Babolat makes rackets that, like other smart sporting goods, leverage accelerometers, gyroscopes, and microprocessors. The racket collects statistics about many things, including shot power, endurance, and technique. Players can learn how often they hit each stroke flat, with topspin, or with slice.[6]

- Fitness Equipment: Technogym provides treadmills, elliptical machines, and exercise bikes that track your workout and provide information to improve your performance. They also offer a cloud-based app that provides customers access to their health data from anywhere and allows them to monitor their fitness activity. Tangram provides jump ropes that count and track jumps.

- Integrated Apps: Under Armour's HealthBox collects data from all wearable and fitness devices and displays the information in a single app. It includes information about sleep, caloric intake, workout recommendations, heart rate, weight, and exercise activity.

Baby Products: Baby monitors have moved beyond the devices that enable you to hear if the baby is crying. You can now purchase a baby sock that monitors a baby's heart rate, breathing, and sleep. There are also onesies equipped with sensors to monitor breathing, movement, respiration patterns, sleep activity, skin temperature, and body position. There are sensor pads that you can put under the mattress to monitor movement and alert you if your baby stops moving for 20 seconds.[7]

Breaker Panels: A sensor from Neurio allows you to control your electricity usage. It can differentiate usage by different appliances so you can pinpoint the main contributors to your electricity bill and perhaps adjust your usage accordingly. It can also recognize and alert you to abnormal situations, such as leaving the oven on for an extended period.[8]

Food containers: Vessyl produces a beverage container that analyzes the ingredients of your drink and lets you know the number of calories, nutritional content, and a hydration capacity of what you are consuming. Neo produces a food container for dry goods, such as oatmeal or rice, that measures how much is left and automatically reorders when your stock is running low.

Ovens: Modern ovens do more than just heat your food so it cooks. The company June produces an oven that recognizes what you are cooking and can modify the temperature when appropriate. For example, it can know when a turkey is cooked and then increase the heat for a few minutes to make it crispy on the outside.[9]

Thermostats: Nest created the category of smart thermostats. Today, smart thermostats allow you to save money on your electricity bill by automatically adjusting temperatures when you are away, adjusting heating and cooling in each room based on whether or not someone is inside it, and enabling remote access via a phone.

Faucets: There are shower faucets that control the temperature to your desired setting. Also, to save water, you can purchase a showerhead that senses your proximity to it and adjusts the water flow in response. For example, stepping back to shampoo your hair reduces the flow, while stepping back in to rinse increases it. Digital-enabled faucets can also track the movement of water and shut off if they sense a leak.

Lawn Sprinkling: Modern lawn sprinkling systems embed digital to undertake tasks such as monitoring weather forecast, diagnosing moisture in the soil, measuring sun exposure, and adjusting the amount of water based on such inputs. The customer gets the desired outcome: a well-watered lawn, at a lower cost since less water is used.

INDUSTRIAL EXAMPLES

There are many industrial examples of embedding digital into products to achieve faster, smarter, better, safer, and more cost-effective outcomes. Here are a few of them:

Industrial Equipment: Fusheng air compressors predict and detect maintenance needs, and arrange for service to the compressor before it fails. *Preventative* maintenance, which involves shutting a machine down to perform the maintenance whether or not it is required, is expensive, causes unnecessary downtime, and consumes labor and spare parts unnecessarily. *Predictive* maintenance, instead, uses sensors to track the condition and usage trends of the components and send the data to applications in the cloud, which then identify whether and when maintenance is required. Companies can also analyze the data to help customers understand how to use the equipment with less energy.

Customers achieve their desired outcomes of using the air compressor with maximum uptime and lowest cost. Fusheng boasts that their products result in a reduction in MTTR (Mean Time to Repair) of 15%, an increase in first-time fix rate of 20% through better data, and a reduction in downtime of 25%.[10]

While this example is restricted to air compressors, companies are taking the same approach to updating most industrial products. Countless industrial products now typically feature sensors, including elevators, cooling and heating systems, oil and gas equipment, motors, material handling, valves, power generation, refrigeration, and robotics.

Agriculture Equipment: Irrigation systems no longer just spray water when instructed. They now make decisions about when and where to dispense water based on many factors, including soil moisture, the needs of the plant, and weather forecasts.

Offices: Building owners are embedding digital throughout offices. Current smart offices may feature any of the following:[11]

- Sensors that detect employees through their phone on arrival and direct them to an available parking spot
- Biometric sensors that recognize employees' faces and permit access through security
- Apps that direct employees to an available workspace or the fastest route to a meeting place
- Wireless charging tables in conference rooms to keep devices from dying and automatic screen sharing to enable smoother collaboration
- Intelligent heating, lighting, and cooling that allows users to rate their comfort levels so that the building learns how to adjust the temperature appropriately
- Pre-ordered lunch in the cafeteria and payment via an app
- IT supplies like power cords and flash drives available from vending machines that bill the department based on recognition from the user's phone

Shipping Containers. Shipping containers are being digitally equipped and connected to enable global, real-time location and status visibility. Container sensors can also monitor for vibrations, attempted burglaries, and traces of substances in the air. They allow remote control of temperature and humidity. The result is a reduction in cargo damage, reduced theft, easier regulatory compliance, and less frequent manual inspections.[12]

Connected Worker: Workers are becoming more digital, and are being equipped with wearable, intelligent sensors to improve their efficiency and safety. For example, sensors can diagnose environmental conditions and alert the worker and a remote office of the danger so the operator can take corrective action. Devices can also notify the people onsite when a dangerous situation arises. Emergency crews can receive orders on wearable devices.

PRODUCT AS A SERVICE

Some companies are leveraging IoT to provide "Product as a Service" and subscription or usage pricing, taking advantage of sensors that can monitor condition and usage. Usage-based pricing is far from new. Xerox pioneered it in the sixties when they discovered that their customers struggled to come up with enough money to buy a photocopier, but were in a position to pay for individual copies. Xerox installed meters to track the number of copies and sales took off. Today, thanks to widespread Internet access, lower cost and higher functionality sensors, and customers' receptivity to the subscription model, the Product-as-a-Service approach is attractive even for smaller assets and smaller units of usage.

The advantages of a Product-as-a-Service model for the customer are not having to come up with the capital up front, the certainty of costs given that the monthly fee includes service and maintenance, and not needing to worry about installation and upgrades. It also contributes to agility, since companies can often begin using the asset sooner, and since the customer does not own the asset, they do not need to track it. With a tight contract, the client has the added advantage of being able to stop using the asset if business conditions change and they no longer need it.

There is a disadvantage to the provider insofar as they are missing the larger up-front revenue that comes from an outright sale. By sacrificing that lump sum, however, the provider gains certain recurring revenue, and the approach naturally creates an active, ongoing customer relationship. Further, the approach provides rich usage and maintenance data that the company would not otherwise have. That data can be fed back to product design and manufacturing departments for continuous product improvement. The information can also contribute to customer success, since the provider may see opportunities for the customer to use the asset better to achieve their desired outcome.

The most common example of Product as a Service is cloud computing, including SaaS, PaaS, and IaaS. However, many industries are adopting the approach, including jet engines, farm equipment, and plant floor equipment. IDC Manufacturing Insights estimates that 40% of Top 100 discrete manufacturers and 20% of Top 100 process manufacturers will provide Product-as-a-Service platforms by 2018.[13]

CONCLUSION

The examples presented in this chapter are to stimulate ideas. If you are a consumer company, do your products share characteristics with window blinds—move automatically based on an external factor (in this case sunlight)? Alternatively, perhaps with light bulbs—a product the consumer would like to control remotely or automatically? Or are they like sports equipment, where collection and analysis of data create enormous value? If you are an industrial company, would your customers appreciate your products monitoring themselves and arranging for service, like Fusheng air compressors? Would they like your products to make decisions, like irrigation systems deciding how much water to dispense? Would they like to be alerted about possible burglaries, like modern shipping containers can do?

While this chapter focused on *providing* digital, Chapter 7 now looks at *using* digital to improve internal processes.

Seven

Digitizing Operational Processes

The business literature is active with books, papers, and blog posts about digital transformation, what it is, and how to achieve it. Normally, they contain anecdotes about what certain companies are doing to adapt to new digital realities. This chapter contains some anecdotes but also strives to present a more holistic view of what a company does and how to leverage digital developments in operational processes (Figure 7-1).

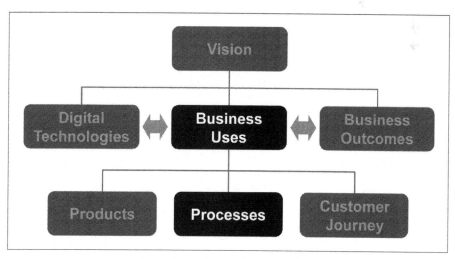

Figure 7-1: Business Uses: Operational Processes

We will cover the eight processes in this chapter. I refer to these as the operational processes.

- Deliver Physical Products and Services
- Develop and Manage Human Capital
- Manage Information Technology
- Manage Financial Resources
- Acquire, Construct, and Manage Assets
- Manage Enterprise Risk, Compliance, Remediation, and Resiliency
- Manage External Relationships
- Develop and Manage Business Capabilities

You can treat this chapter as a reference, consulting only the sections about processes that are important to you.

DELIVER PHYSICAL PRODUCTS AND SERVICES

Competing in Third Digital requires determining how you will digitize production to meet customer expectations for lower prices, faster time to market, and customization. McKinsey estimates the following benefits are possible by digitizing the supply chain:[1]

- 30–50% reduction of total machine downtime
- 45–55% increase in technical professions through automation of knowledge work
- Inventory holding costs decreased by 20–50%
- 20–50% reduction in time to market
- 10–40% reduction in maintenance costs
- Productivity increase from 3–5%

Production starts with planning and forecasting. Companies are using computer learning to improve forecasting and demand planning, and, consequently, fill rates. Computer learning can model the causes of demand variation and learn the potential impacts on demand from pro-motions, seasonality, weather conditions, and many other factors.

To make things, you have to buy things. How actively are procurement or-ganizations pursuing digital transformation? In their 2016 Chief Procurement Officer Survey, Deloitte Consulting discovered that 60% of companies do not have a digital strategy for procurement.[2] This is an area that will need more attention as companies undertake digital transformation.

Moving to production, one of the most significant trends is the in-creased use of robotics. With advances in mechanical dexterity, machine learning, and material science, robots are taking on jobs that were not possible a few years ago. On the manufacturing floor, robots are welding, assembling, machining, and performing tasks too dangerous for humans.

According to data from the International Federation of Robots (IFR), the worldwide sales of industrial robots achieved a record 248,000 units in 2015, continuing a global automation boom. The sales figures for in-dustrial robots have increased almost four-fold since 2009, and IFR ex-pects that there is no end in sight, with some 2.3 million units expected to be deployed on factory floors by 2018.[3] The largest sales growth, at 15%, is in the USA, and the biggest industry is automotive, accounting for about half of all robots sold.

Companies are particularly interested in the cost reductions enabled by robotics. Until recently, many of the manufacturing cost reductions were achieved by offshoring production. However, the financial advan-tages of offshoring are dwindling as wages in the offshore countries are going up. For example, since 2001, average hourly wages in China have increased 12% per year.[4] Bringing production back to North America by leveraging robotics has been dubbed "cybershoring." In addition to cutting costs, cybershoring creates useful information. When third party offshore companies perform production, access to information is more challenging than when the company performs the manufacturing itself.

The way companies maintain their production facilities is changing. Plant maintenance has been, historically, mostly reactive. With reactive maintenance, when a machine breaks, the factory dispatches a service call and technicians come and fix it. This approach yields a costly production slowdown while the machine is out of service. Preventative maintenance helps this by arranging for planned shutdown to replace parts that may break, but, as discussed earlier, if the original parts would not have actually failed, preventative maintenance incurs unnecessary cost in labor, downtime, and replacement parts. Moving to predictive maintenance, wherein sensors in the machines or parts monitor the condition of the part and predict when maintenance is required, is more efficient and effective.

Warehousing and logistics are also evolving. In warehouses, companies are using headsets that provide instructions in the picker's visual field, which frees up their hands to do the actual picking. Robots are also now being used to pick, pack, palletize, load, and unload.

In the area of outbound logistics, big data analysis is helping with route optimization. Also, adaptive cruise control in trucks is improving safety. These controls automatically maintain safe distances between trucks and other vehicles. Third Digital technology is also enabling shipping containers to be tracked more closely to isolate bottlenecks, shrinkage, or disruption.

Still, on the topic of outbound logistics, companies, especially B2C ones, are increasingly expected to provide same-day delivery. Amazon is contributing significantly to these demands. They continue to add cities in which Amazon Prime customers can receive same-day delivery at no additional cost. Always pushing the limits, they introduced Prime Now service in 2015, which provides one-hour delivery. Their Prime Air service—deliveries by drones—once approved, will deliver in thirty minutes or less.

The Austrian grocer Billa has offered same-day delivery since 2014, delivered to home lockboxes through their partnership with Lockbox. Lockbox signs up consumers and provides them with an "anchor," a small device attached to their front door. Retailers can pack deliveries into a secure box, deliver it to the consumer's home, and lock it to the anchor. The customer does not pay for the lockbox service and pays regular prices from the retailers. Billa fulfills the orders from their stores, treating them like extended warehouses.[5]

Same-day delivery is not just a threat; it is also an opportunity. The World Economic Forum expects there is an additional $30 billion of profit opportunity from premiums consumers are willing to pay for same-day service. The increased demand for same-day deliveries may increase the portion from the current 5% of all deliveries to 40% by 2025.

Organizations are using delivery drones commercially. DHL has been delivering small packages via drones since 2014.[6] They started with the German island Juist, then extended the number of locations and advanced the drones themselves. They are now using their Parcelcoptor 3.0, which is able to be automatically loaded and unloaded and to fly through harsh weather conditions. The payloads were most often urgently needed medicines or sporting goods. To ensure success, they partnered with the Ministry of Transportation, which established a restricted flight zone for DHL.[7]

Drone delivery has been active in China since 2013. SF Express, the country's largest mail carrier, began in the city of Dongguang. They now deliver in several cities in southern and eastern China, using a fleet of over 1,000 drones. Alibaba has also been experimenting with drone deliveries.[8]

Amazon has filed a patent to 3D-print products in their delivery trucks to further reduce the time between placement of the order and delivery of the product—essentially making the products *while* delivering them. Google also received a patent for an autonomous delivery truck. The vehicles will include lockers, which the recipient will unlock with a code they receive.[9]

Autonomous vehicles are not limited to the last mile. They have been in commercial use in the USA since May 2015, when the State of Nevada Department of Motor Vehicles approved the Daimler Inspiron truck for service on public highways. The rules require that a driver be present and that the driver takes over when getting on or off the highways or driving on smaller roads. There are many expected benefits from self-driving trucks: fewer accidents, less CO_2 emission, and lower costs from better mileage.

DEVELOP AND MANAGE HUMAN CAPITAL

Many of the factors driving change in customer expectations are also driving change in employee expectations. Like customers, employees are connected and sharing. They expect consumer-grade systems and tools and plan to bring in their own devices. They want to associate with a brand whose reputation aligns with their values. They expect their employers to be digitally progressive. They have blurred lines between professional and private lives. They expect personalized learning and development opportunities. They expect the ability to work anywhere, at least occasionally.

These expectations are not only prevalent in millennials. The older workers have similar expectations. Interestingly, the workforce is getting younger and older at the same time. The groups of employees who are under 25 and those over 45 are growing, while the 25–45 group is shrinking. Managing human capital in the digital world is not just about catering to young people.

HR plays a critical role in driving digital capabilities throughout the company. HR helps managers look for and assess digital skills in candidates in all functions. Further, HR is assisting those in other functions to understand the non-technical skills that are required to succeed in the digital world: adaptability, social collaboration, the expectation for automation, and communication. They are also playing a leading role in helping companies re-organize for digital—identifying the capabilities required and how the company should be organized to provide them.

Almost every role requires some degree of digital literacy; therefore, companies must build digital capabilities into every competency model. Workers on the factory floor need it so they can suggest manufacturing improvements. Senior leadership overseeing any function requires it to lead and operate their functions—much like they need to know how to read, write, do math, and interact with each other. Since digital technology and processes are so pervasive, so too must be digital knowledge.

Let's follow human resource management through from hiring to retiring.

Recruitment and job searches have changed. One-quarter of all job applications in North America come from mobile devices. Seventy-three percent of people 18–34 found their last job through a social network.[10] Eighty-nine percent of all recruiters have hired someone through LinkedIn.[11] Companies looking to win the war for talent are recruiting where the candidates are. They are also better able to improve the likelihood of selecting candidates who will succeed, using analytics and AI to associate better data collected during the recruiting process with on-the-job success.

Most resume screening is done by computers, using algorithms. A new ethical and legal risk is emerging: algorithms that inadvertently discriminate. A recent startup audits algorithms for discrimination—O'Neil Risk Consulting & Algorithmic Auditing—founded by Cathy O'Neil, who authored the book *Weapons of Math Destruction*, a fascinating look at the risks of discrimination in the algorithms being used not only for job applications but credit applications and even prison sentences.

Human capital management also includes attracting and managing temporary workers. On-demand, contract, or "gig" labor has increased significantly. Using non-employee workers contributes to companies' agility and ability to access specialized skills and knowledge. Intuit estimates that by 2020, 40% of the workforce will be contingent.

Once recruited, development and counseling start. Development and feedback are now happening on an ongoing basis, rather than forced once or twice per year. As companies move faster and with more agility, so too are the performance management systems. A new breed of social performance management (SPM) tool has emerged, like Salesforce's *work.com*, which enables users to align goals, performance, and real-time recognition and rewards.

Employee development must address the digital transformation skills gaps. A recent study by SAP shows that companies are not making much progress in this respect. It found that only 27% of respondents in the survey thought their business executives had the skills necessary for digital transformation and only 10% of the respondents said the HR function had a recruitment/training program to close the skill gap.[12] Come on, companies! Without digital skills, how can you survive in the digital world?

Employee relations is going digital as labor organizations begin to embrace digital technology. The 2015 movement advocating a $15 minimum wage used social media to mobilize thousands of fast food workers. It was effective: several cities increased their minimum wages because of pressure and protest. New York State will require fast food companies to pay workers a minimum of $15 per hour by 2021.[13]

The HR function is the most advanced function on moving applications to the cloud. Deployment of cloud solutions for HR is also helping to force simpler processes and more commonality across multiple divisions of a company.

HR departments are also making use of predictive analytics to create insights into the talent on hand. Leading companies mine existing HR data. For example, Dow Chemical combed through historical data on its 40,000 employees to identify workforce needs segmented by age groups, job levels, and business units. The model includes internal factors such as attrition and promotions and external factors such as political and legal considerations. Using this analysis, Dow can better anticipate and plan for the impact of events such as facility closures or industry slowdowns and upswings.[14]

Just as companies are providing personalized service to customers and are working to improve customer engagement, they are providing personalized talent management to employees and working to measure and improve employee engagement. Given the war for talent, the marketing aspect of human capital management is increasingly prominent. Companies are encouraging executives to engage with news media as well as be active on social media to get the brand message out, which helps with recruiting and retention. Companies are using sensing tools to understand what is being said and felt about them as employers, similar to the customer sentiment analysis that has become standard.

Many Generation Y workers—those born in the eighties and nineties—join organizations whom they believe contribute in some positive way to the world. Therefore, communications from the company need to include messages that speak to those values. If external and internal communications are only about business numbers, retaining Gen Y employees will be more difficult.

Retirement is also transforming. Companies are leveraging analytics to predict the number of retirements they will have each year. Predictions are based on the demographics of their existing workforce, but also on factors such as the strength of the economy and the potential value of 401K plans. These predictions help companies avoid being caught unprepared for a surge in retirements.

MANAGE INFORMATION TECHNOLOGY

Information Technology (IT) processes play a leading role in digital transformation. In this section, we examine the current IT state that most companies find themselves in; how to improve the current state to enable digital initiatives; required IT capabilities; security; information management; and building, delivering, and supporting IT solutions in the context of the new digital era.

Imagine a CEO of a $10 billion company asked you what the IT function should look like. How likely is it you would say something like the following?

"Ms. CEO, you should hire a large team to build hundreds of different proprietary applications that don't talk to each other. The applications do not have to share technology or have similar underlying technologies, like consistent databases. The large team will stay in place to support the applications. You should then purchase hundreds of commercial applications that again don't talk to each other and don't share technology. Be ready to pay exorbitant maintenance and service fees to the vendors forever.

The applications should be difficult to use and should look nothing like the intuitive applications that your employees use outside the office. One of these—let's call it ERP—should be huge, difficult to change, and make digital initiatives more difficult. It will contain data desperately needed by customer-facing applications, but not accessible to them.

You should buy lots of servers to run all this software and set up big rooms to house them. You'll want to hire even more people to run the servers and the network that connects them to the users. At some point, you may want to outsource this big environment and lock yourself into a long-term, fixed contract. Then you will not be able to leverage lower-cost on-demand computing like your nimbler competitors.

The skills of your IT people should be in operating this outdated environment. Projects should take a long time to complete and, by the time they are finished, will serve requirements that are no longer relevant.

Plan on spending more than $100 million per year to do all this. Do not plan on having much money left over for innovation or digital projects. Since this environment will be broad and complex, you will not have the ability to change quickly to meeting customer demands."

You get the picture. No one in their right mind would recommend this type of IT environment, but sadly, it is fairly accurate for most companies. An IT strategy that is basically the opposite of the one above is required to support digital transformation. Companies should include elements of the following in their IT strategy:

- Simplify business processes
- Reduce the number of applications
- Fit applications and technology together through enterprise architecture

- Move to cloud (off-premise) and leverage commercial software
- Create an agile IT environment and delivery capability
- Establish a culture of innovation and partnership with the business
- Leverage partners
- Recruit and develop digital talent

Most companies' IT strategies include a plan to continually chip away at the IT debt to free up resources to work on digital initiatives.

IT functions recognize that capabilities are needed from two perspectives: business innovation and business optimization. Business innovation refers to fundamental changes to the company's products, processes, or customer journey. Optimization refers to operating the business efficiently within the context of its existing products, services, and processes.

The current state of data in most companies inhibits their ability to execute digital initiatives. Frequently, the required data is just not available or is tough to retrieve. Companies are dealing with this by investing in data virtualization. This approach allows applications or services to get information in real-time from other applications, without knowing the format or structure of the underlying data source. Implementing a virtualized information access layer provides a consistent view and ready access to operational data, regardless of where the data resides.

Digital transformation requires solutions to be built or acquired and deployed more quickly and frequently than in the past. Moreover, the lifetime of solutions is shorter. Companies capable of faster software delivery that incorporates ongoing customer feedback have a marked advantage, given rapidly changing customer and market requirements. To deliver, IT functions are moving away from traditional IT governance, which was designed for traditional IT processes: build, support, and maintain infrastructure and systems. These conventional methods are giving way to agile processes that make IT nimbler, enabling it to keep pace with and drive digital transformation.

Companies are moving support of traditional applications to Centers of Expertise (CoE) to focus available resources on digital initiatives.

Particularly for companies that contain multiple business units, moving legacy system support from the business unit to a central CoE provides economies of scale and frees the business unit resources to execute digital initiatives.

Achieving digital transformation initiatives requires the IT function to shift their role from just delivering technology solutions to being trusted advisors who help business partners through digital business changes. As such, they realize that new skills and talents are required. Business skills are needed, as are technical skills, in such areas as social media, mobile, big data, IoT, and enterprise architecture. Companies are using several of the following approaches to get the required skills in the fastest manner:

- Building internally—driving skill improvements with existing staff
- Recruiting from outside—raising the profile to attract talent
- Acqui-hires—strategic acquisitions to bring in talent
- Partnering—leveraging other firms who already have the experience and talent

Some companies are spinning off the digital initiatives into a separate organization with a culture more aligned with the required skills in order to improve the effectiveness of skill-building. Companies are also generating excitement about their digital initiatives by creating visibility through publications and other media. Whereas previously, speaking to the press or elaborating on social media may have seemed self-serving for CIOs, in today's war on talent, it is a necessary part of generating interest in the company and its initiatives.

MANAGE FINANCIAL RESOURCES

Historically, the role of Finance has been to perform general accounting and handle the budget, payroll, accounts payable, statutory reporting, treasury, taxes, and global trade. For several decades, companies have been meeting these needs by deploying traditional systems such as ERP. Automation continues, especially the deployment of robotic process automation to further automate the processing work involved in areas like accounts payable, expense reimbursement, and payroll.

The larger evolution, though, is delivering analytical insights, business intelligence, and intangible assets. The value of intangible assets such as analytical capability, brand, customer loyalty, IP (patents and copyrights), and human resources is increasing. An annual survey conducted by Ocean Tomo, a firm that provides advisory services on intellectual property, shows that in 1985, investors put 32% of their valuation on intangible components and 68% on tangible components (property, plant, and equipment). In 2015, the figures had practically been reversed: investors put 84% of their valuation on intangibles and only 16% on tangible assets.[15]

Since the Finance function plays a large role in allocating capital, financial planning and budgeting processes are evolving in the digital world to ensure that the initiatives and projects that drive value in intangibles are prioritized equally or higher than those that drive the value of tangibles. Further, finance functions are moving beyond the reporting of financial data to also include reporting KPIs that convey the more current value, such as customer engagement, efficiency, traffic, cost per transaction, intangible assets, and digital revenue.

Like all functions, Finance is developing the ability to reduce cycle time and improve agility as these are increasingly required in the digital world. Rapid decision-making enabled by immediate access to a single source of truth is becoming more common. Several financial attributes are moving closer to real time, including cash flow forecasting, slice and dice analysis, and even closing the books.

As the transactional work becomes more digitized, freeing up people to work on more value-added activities, like planning and analysis, the skill sets required in Finance will trend more toward data science, analysis, and business planning.

Machine learning and NLP will play a bigger role in financial processes. Auditors are leveraging Natural language processing for document reviews since computers can now understand the unstructured data, such as text, better than they could a few years ago. Companies are also leveraging technology to find value in narrative data and combining such data with quantitative data. Machine learning is being deployed to analyze multiple indicators to improve forecasts, since computers are better than humans at sifting through vast amounts of data to find patterns and test hypotheses. Computers will also allow more granular, rather than aggregate, analyses.

ACQUIRE, CONSTRUCT, AND MANAGE ASSETS

Improving asset performance and reducing asset costs are part of the move toward operational efficiencies that enable the lower prices that digital customers have come to expect. Customers today have less tolerance for the additional costs incurred by unplanned outages, underperforming assets, and high maintenance requirements—inefficiencies that are reflected in prices to the customers.

It is the *management* of physical assets, more than their acquisition and construction, which has the greatest impact from digital technology. As was seen in the description of IoT, digitization enables companies to monitor assets more carefully, enabling predictive, rather than preventative, maintenance. Applying the digital technologies will reduce costs of the assets while increasing reliability and performance.

A component of managing assets is plant maintenance. A good example of digitizing plant maintenance is Exelon, the largest private operator of nuclear power plants in the United States. They developed a mobile system to digitize plant maintenance completely. Because of the stringent regulations and safety requirements surrounding nuclear power, work packages in nuclear power plants have been slow to move away from paper. Exelon's system is mobile (tablet-based), incorporates video documentation, enables digital data capture at the source, and integrates fully with existing systems. The workers involved are all connected. Field workers use the tablet to review plans, enter data, and photograph an asset and work real-time with an engineering team that leverages big data analytics to determine a resolution. The system and associated process changes reduced overhead by 50%, generated 1.5 hours per worker per day of available time, reduced rework, and improved productivity of the planners by 30%.[16]

Companies also now have substantially more digital assets to manage, such as documents, images, video, and audio. There are many digital asset management systems on the market that help store, organize, find, and share digital assets. These have become a necessity given the increasing number of digital assets that companies generate.

MANAGE ENTERPRISE RISK, COMPLIANCE, REMEDIATION, AND RESILIENCY

As digital initiatives increase, so does the security risk. IoT opens the risk to all things connected to the Internet. *Harvard Business Review* goes so far as to state that "the functioning of society's infrastructure and our access to sufficient energy depend on our establishment of new cyber security regimes oriented to the internet of things."[17]

Further, cyber-attacks can now have physical consequences. The Stuxnet computer worm that infected industrial sites in Iran attacked the controllers of the centrifuges in a uranium enrichment plant, causing the centrifuges to begin malfunctioning without any apparent reason. *The New York Times* reported that the USA and Israel were responsible for Stuxnet.[18] Separately, in January 2016, 225,000 people in the Ukraine lost power from a cyber attack on the Ukrainian power grid.[19] Cybersecurity researchers in the USA claim to have taken control of a car remotely.

The frequency and severity of cyber-attacks by organizations and nation states will continue to increase. The United States of America's Central Intelligence Agency (CIA) concluded in December 2016 that people with connections to the Russian government obtained emails from the Democratic National Committee and provided them to WikiLeaks with the intention of helping Donald Trump win the election over Hillary Clinton. An attack with the intention of influencing an American election is a big deal and is reflective of the new world in which we live.

Ransomware—situations in which hackers take control of your device and release it back to you for a fee—is increasing. The FBI reports that organizations paid a total of $25 million in ransom in 2015, and $200 million in just the first three months of 2016.[20] Ransomware perpetrators are unlikely to stop at computers and phones; they are likely to target wearables, including medical devices.

Cyber security now must be a top priority for all companies, not only for their internal operations but also for their commercial products that include a digital component. The majority of enterprises have a Chief Information Security Officer (CISO) in place, many of whom report directly to the CEO. Companies should conduct a thorough security review at least once per year. Many companies are doing it twice per year, alternating between security firms to get different perspectives. An important part of addressing the threat is also providing ongoing security training for every employee.

In the area of compliance, banks are using NLP and machine learning to automate compliance to deal with increasing regulatory requirements. These types of artificial intelligence are helping track money laundering, sanction list monitoring, and billing fraud.[21] Companies are moving toward automated and continuous monitoring and the ability to report compliance at any moment. Dashboards include real-time analytics on enterprise risk and compliance.

Regulatory and legal requirements are on the increase. Having more digital assets means more tracking of those assets. Records management requirements include digital as well as physical assets. The SMAC technologies, the rapid pace of innovation, and the increased collaboration with external parties have all complicated risk and compliance management.

MANAGE EXTERNAL RELATIONSHIPS

This process includes building investor, government, and industry relationships as well as managing public relations.

In the digital world, external relationships are more important than ever. Companies are partnering with government organizations to contribute to and deploy technological research, with customers to co-develop new products, and with suppliers to drive efficiencies. Steve Case, in his book *The Third Wave,* states that "If you cannot figure out how to work with government—and how to get government to work with you—you are likely not going to be a successful."[22] Case goes on to say that government—either by action or inaction—defines the environment in which business operates. We cannot underestimate the role that government had in enabling the digital world—for example, placing the Internet in private hands and opening it up to the public and driving the research that created technologies we take for granted today, such as GPS, microchips, and radar.

The digital world also requires companies to create online content to be consumed by investors. Like customers, investors are always online and always sharing. If you have only a small presence in the online world, then other parties—bloggers, analysts, reporters—can take control of your message. Online messaging is now part of public relations. Companies combine traditional PR with online PR—videos, tweets, reviews, and Search Engine Optimization, and blog posts to present information and create conversations. The tone of the online messaging is more personal and the content more helpful than traditional press releases.

DEVELOP AND MANAGE BUSINESS CAPABILITIES

This process includes managing business processes, projects, quality, and change, as well as environmental health and safety risks and programs.

Until recently, process re-engineering was driven primarily by moving your processes to the best practices represented in the software (usually ERP) that you were implementing. You then had to live with those processes for several years. That is no longer the case. Processes need to change too quickly. In Third Digital, all processes need to be digitized to the fullest extent possible. Customers are not prepared to wait for human intervention. Imagine trying to order something and having to wait for a person to check inventory before you could place the order. Also, all processes need to be the most efficient in the world. Customers are not willing to pay more to cover inefficient processes. Back-end process improvement includes determining what steps and decisions can be automated. For customer-facing processes, the additional requirement is to provide the option of self-service wherever possible.

Like process management, project management is changing to accommodate the speed of digital projects. Companies are shifting to Agile project methodology and away from the traditional Waterfall approach. With Waterfall, the project objective and specification are defined, then each phase— design, build, implement—flows to the next. In Agile, the focus is to deliver small chunks of the end product. The project performs design, build, and implement, not sequentially, but in cycles, allowing the project to adapt to changing requirements. Agile is better suited to the rapid innovation, try, and pivot world of digital.

While project management deals with specific projects, portfolio management deals with identifying and managing the best set or portfolio of projects. With the need to move quickly toward digital transformation and the difficulty of identifying clear ROIs for some digital projects, companies are dividing their project portfolios into two parts: Business Optimization and Business Innovation. Business Optimization projects go through more traditional funding and prioritization, while Business Innovation projects are prioritized more by achieving a business outcome that is not necessarily financial in nature, at least not in the short term, such as customer engagement or embedding digital into an existing product.

Digital projects require change management since change now happens more frequently and is more profound. Digital technology is changing the way we work. Advanced automation is introducing new jobs and eliminating old jobs. Managing the change effectively is more important than ever. A leading practice is to assign a senior executive, usually titled the Chief Digital Officer (CDO), to drive the digital transformation and associated change management full-time.

The CDO is someone who has respect from other senior leaders and from lower levels. They know the business well, collaborate internally and externally, and have a firm understanding of digital technology. Leading companies realize that there are several aspects to the change. First, engaging the leadership and employees is critical. While some employees are reluctant to change, many employees embrace the move to digital, because they want to be part of a progressive company.

As companies define digital initiatives and execute projects, they understand that digitization enables a higher level of quality. The use of robots to automate manufacturing and other processes can deliver outcomes more consistently and within a tighter set of specifications. Machine vision is also being deployed to inspect products at various stages in the production line. Big data can be leveraged to analyze machine outputs to identify and repair production faults. Sensors in fabrication machines, like in other assets, can report issues or variabilities outside the norm, allowing the company to fix them before they affect the quality of the end product.

In the area of environment, health, and safety (EHS), digital transformation represents both new risks to be managed and better ways to manage those risks. Regulatory compliance tasks are being automated to improve and streamline compliance functions. EHS incident management process can benefit from digital transformation by systematizing the incident tracking, reporting, root cause analyses, corrective actions, sharing of lessons learned, and implementing preventive actions. Companies that proactively track, report, and share environment, social, and governance (ESG) data and performance information with stakeholders can generate a competitive edge and fortify their social license to operate. TransCanada Pipelines learned the hard way when their proposed pipeline failed to gain regulator permission in the US. Proactive communication of the pipeline's ESG benefits over rail and tanker transportation of oil could have saved this project. Products and processes that leverage new technologies, such as moving robots, introduce new risks. Effective EHS will involve managing these new risks.

Digital allows companies to move beyond lagging EHS indicators to predictive ones. A leading use case is to install sensors in assets that could become unsafe, have the sensors monitor the assets, leverage big data and predictive analytics to assess the safety of the asset, and undertake maintenance or other proactive measures to make the assets safe. Manufacturers with real-time visibility into EHS metrics have a 21% improvement in Overall Equipment Effectiveness.[23] Besides monitoring the assets, sensors can monitor the environment, air quality, and noise levels. Wearables also provide the opportunity to predict medical emergencies or conditions in people so help can be dispatched more quickly.

Using advanced analytics to inform EHS will show patterns and higher risk situations, so that companies can address them. For example, Ann Klee, Vice President Environment, Health & Safety at GE states that "In 2015, GE generated 3.5 million EHS data records to support compliance and operational obligations. We are now combining that data with a huge stream of other information (about weather, business activity, etc.) and using data visualization and analytics tools. This provides risk managers with real-time, actionable insights about our highest risks and allows for more efficient resource allocation and risk control."[24]

CONCLUSION

Despite its length relative to others, this chapter represented only a tiny portion of the opportunities to digitize operational processes. You can find more imformation about the digitization of operational processes in the accompanying website *www.thirddigital.com*.

Another note: While this chapter covers the full set of operational processes, no company would want to tackle digital projects in all or most processes. Chapter 9 lays out approaches to prioritizing and focusing digital efforts.

We have looked at providing digital as part of a product or service offered and using digital to improve operational processes. Chapter 8 explores using and providing digital to improve your customer's journey.

Eight

Improving the
Customer Journey

This chapter deals with improving the customer journey (Figure 8-1).

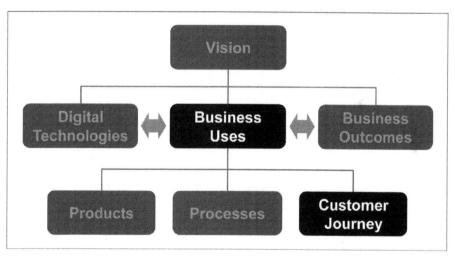

Figure 8-1: Business Uses: Customer Journey

The customer journey is the set of steps a customer undertakes to find, order, pay for, receive, use, and share information about your product. These steps may involve multiple touchpoints through various channels and across many devices. One of the three business uses of digital is to make the customer journey easier and the entire experience better. Today, customers expect that whatever they have to do will be fast and easy. They expect continuous improvement in the customer journey. They also expect an integrated experience across all channels. If the company does not provide a fast, easy, and enjoyable experience that continuously gets better, it will lose customers.

JOURNEY MAPPING

Journey mapping is becoming an increasingly common approach to understanding customers in Third Digital. A journey map outlines a customer's expectations and experiences throughout the multiple steps at which they interact with your company and with others, from evaluating offerings, to selecting, purchasing, using, receiving service, and discussing their experience with others. Customer journey mapping includes defining the customer touchpoints and the content for each touchpoint.

Journey maps for B2B companies are typically more complex than for B2C companies because there are usually more people involved in the evaluation, selection, and use of the product.

Let's consider a real example of a journey map. The software company SAS created a journey map that they use to tailor the information content and format they provide to individual clients, based on the stage of their journey. They break down the customer journey, and their method of reaching the customer throughout the journey, into the following six stages:[1]

- Need—High-level messaging, including thought leadership strategies (articles, blog posts). Content at this phase explains the problem and provides a path forward.
- Research—Content that validates the customer's need to solve the problem. Material here focuses on specific business issues and includes third-party resources (analyst reviews, research reports).
- Decide—Deeper content that provides more product-specific information. This material validates the proposed solution through customer success stories, research reports, product fact sheets.

- Adopt—Onboarding and self-service content. This stage focuses on introducing customers to support resources and online communities as well as "do-it-yourself" material that introduces the customer to the solution.
- Use—Content, such as advanced educational information, user conferences, and product-specific webinars. At this stage, users mature with their use of technology and turn to more technical resources to expand their knowledge.
- Recommend—Content specific to extending the relationship with the customer, including speaking opportunities, focus group participation and sales references, as well as involvement in cross- and up-sell opportunities.

The map for your customers would be different from this one. The first step in improving the customer journey is to define your map through customer interviews, discussions, and internal information, such as transactions, Web page logs, and interviews with employees who interact with customers.

Once the journey is mapped, the task is to identify the following:

- How can we make the journey easier and more enjoyable for customers, including developing community and engagement?
- What are all the interactions that customer use—with you, your competitors, their friends, online, or anywhere else?
- How can we provide what they expect in each of the interactions that we can influence?
- What is the outcome or destination desired by the customers, and how can we best get them there?

Improving the journey may also involve modifying your value proposition or even your pricing approach. The value proposition is how your product or service solves the customer's problem and delivers benefits—how, in other words, your product is valuable to the customer. Companies are adapting to Third Digital by redefining their value proposition by adding digital content, developing communities, and improving engagement. Consider the example from Chapter 5 where NIKE's annual report talked far more about community and engagement than shoes and apparel.

Aligned with the move to providing Products as a Service, companies are experimenting with alternative pricing strategies, such as subscription models that charge customers a monthly or usage-based fee. More and more, customers want an outcome but don't necessarily want to own the product that gets them that outcome. They may, for example, opt not to buy a car and, instead, use Uber or Car2Go for transportation.

Let's look at a couple more examples of how companies worked on the customer journey and the impact. Sungevity is a provider of solar panels for homes. However, they state their mission with a focus on customer experience: "We are building the world's most energized network of customers who power their lives with sunshine." Their customer journey work yielded the following steps for making customers aware of Sungevity and turning them into satisfied users:[2]

- They send a mailing to targeted homeowners. The mailing contains a URL that goes to a page with an image of the homeowner's house with solar panels superimposed on the roof, so the owner can see what their home would look like with solar panels. The page also contains a link so the prospect can see what their potential savings would be. Even this initial outreach is customized, and it fuses physical (hardcopy mailing) with digital (link to a Web page).
- The customized Web page also includes a link to connect with a live sales agent. When the prospect connects, the Web page that the prospect is viewing is also displayed to the sales agent. Upon completion of the call, the agent sends the prospect videos with more information.
- After the call, the agent sends an email to nearby customers who have agreed to act as references, along with their phone numbers.

- The next time the prospect calls the agent or visits the Web page, the site has a tailored lease ready to go. The prospect can click to connect with an agent who will explain the lease and answer any questions.
- When the prospect decides to proceed, they provide an e-signature.
- Once signed, when the customer visits the site subsequently, Sungevity provides them with information about the progress of permits and installation, which refreshes as staff enter new information.
- Once installed, the customer receives reports on energy generated and savings, which reinforces their decision to buy.

Notice how Sungevity makes it easy and exciting to move customers along to the next steps (customized Web pages, click to call, lease ready to go)?

Bombardier Recreational Products, manufacturers of snowmobiles, personal watercraft, and all-terrain vehicles, set customer journey improvement as a strategic priority. The employees had passion for improving the customer experience, so it was a matter of focusing that passion. They spent several months speaking with customers and defined five top priorities in the customer journey: trial, delivery, service, rider community, and product experience. They called each of these priorities a Moment of Truth (MoT) and assigned teams to improve each MoT. The teams examined all available data and made a point to interview dissatisfied customers each month. The Delivery team also interviewed their dealers. In their words, they transformed the delivery experience from "Here are your keys, please sign" to a "Wow" experience that builds the customer's confidence and excitement. They continue to work to continuously improve all MoTs.[3]

UNDERSTANDING MODERN CUSTOMERS

Companies are moving beyond looking at segments of customers based on demographics such as age and gender, and have begun addressing customers in segments of one: understanding individual customers, their purchase history, and their preferences, across all channels. Companies are also working to understand the digital behavior of their customers, including analyzing social media activity. More and more, the sensors embedded into products as part of IoT are providing information not only about the product but also about the ways customers use it.

Understanding customers includes understanding how much "digital" they want and where. Customers often are happy to receive the well-timed, personal offers that are only possible through digital technology. However, when it comes to resolving issues, a recent Accenture study showed that 83% of customers prefer dealing with people than computers on customer service matters. This issue is not small: more than half of consumers have switched providers within a year because of unsatisfactory customer service, and the cost of the switching totals $1.6 trillion.[4]

IMPROVING THE CUSTOMER EXPERIENCE

The customer journey translates to an overall customer experience. Understanding the customer experience across the journey, from selecting, to using, to recommending, enables you to understand where the experience can be improved.

A good example is the NFL. In 2014, they recognized that millennials—on whom they depend for a future audience—were not going to games, primarily because of the lack of WiFi in stadiums. It was painful for these folks to be disconnected from full use of the Internet for several hours or to consume their data to do what they like to do at events, such as posting pictures and videos to social media. Rising ticket prices and dropping large-screen television prices made this problem even worse.

The NFL, along with other major sports leagues, responded by installing high-speed WiFi in their stadiums. As part of the customer experience improvement, they also developed apps that offer discounted seat upgrades upon entrance, show instant replays, take food and drink orders, enable the purchase of tickets for future games, and even show wait times for the nearest restrooms.[5]

Over the last two years, as these features became commonplace, expectations from fans in all age groups rose. They now expect this type of enhanced experience at all stadiums. Those that don't provide it are at a significant disadvantage—a good example of how rising expectations makes it necessary to keep up with digital initiatives, especially those that have such a direct impact on the customer.

To determine their customers' needs and wants, in addition to mapping the customer journey through the lifecycle, companies are getting customer feedback wherever possible, and monitoring social media. Companies are also building feedback loops from Customer Success teams since the Customer Success function works directly with the customers to help them achieve their desired outcomes. Detailed analytics around clicks and online behavior is standard, and so are site traffic patterns, usability tests, and customer surveys.

Predominantly physical companies have a natural disadvantage when it comes to acquiring customer information since the use of their product does not leave a digital trail. They are compensating for this by deploying digital technologies to get as close as they can to creating a digital trail. They may, for example, use machine vision to see who is coming into their stores, gather demographic information such as approximate age and gender, see in which aisles they travel, and compare that data to their purchases to see whether there are patterns that enable the retailers to improve the customer experience.

MARKETING WITHIN THE JOURNEY

Marketing will continue to undergo substantive changes to align with the evolving customer journey. For one, marketing continues to move to digital, as evidenced by how companies are allocating and spending their marketing budgets. Digital marketing budgets are steadily increasing, while budgets for traditional marketing are being cut down. The 2016 CMO Survey, a biannual survey sponsored by Deloitte, American Marketing Association, and Duke University, gathered the following statistics:[6]

- Spending on traditional advertising has been decreasing at an average rate of 2.5% per year for over the last two years, while spending on digital marketing has been increasing at an average rate of 12.7% per year.
- Marketing budgets as a percent of total budgets rose from 10.9% in 2014 to 12.1% in 2016.
- Marketing budget as a percent of company budget also differs according to the amount of Internet sales the company does. For companies that do less than 10% of their sales over the Internet, marketing is 11.5% of total company budget; for those that do more than 10% of their sales on the Internet, marketing is 16.8% of total budget.
- Social media spending is currently 10.6% of marketing budgets. Companies surveyed expect that to increase to 20.9% over the next five years.
- Companies surveyed expect the portion of marketing allocated to mobile to roughly triple from 5.9% to 14.6%.
- The portion of marketing spent on marketing analytics is expected to approximately double over the next three years from 6.7% to 11.1%

The bulk of digital marketing budgets is allocated to search marketing ($32B in the USA in 2015), display advertising ($24B), social media ($10B), and email marketing ($2B).

Marketers now have better visibility into their marketing spending, which enables them to allocate more of their budget to higher-performing approaches. Gaining useful analytic information takes some work. You must first prepare the data for analysis, which involves collecting it at all points of the customer journey, keeping it clean, identifying data across multiple sources and multiple contact points that pertain to a single customer, and attaching all those disconnected pieces of data to individual customers. Then, you have to look for patterns of customer action, the information they received, whether or not a sale occurred, and the type and size of the sale. When the software company SAS went through this exercise, they learned that they were sending early customer journey messages to customers who had already purchased. SAS developed a better understanding of where each customer was in the journey and was able to tailor their messages and information to each specific stage.

Analytics are also helping marketers identify specific promotions presented to individual customers, and track customer responses to the promotions so they can adjust and make them more effective.

Companies are simultaneously employing outbound and inbound marketing strategies. Inbound attempts to attract customers to the company's online spaces, and its key methods, include social, Search Engine Optimization, and Pay per Click. Outbound, on the hand, is the more traditional approach of trying to reach customers in their own spaces. It includes email campaigns; tradeshows; press releases; webinars; and print, radio, and billboard advertising. On average, 44% of marketing budgets are spent on inbound, while 48% is dedicated to outbound.[7]

In recognition of the importance of digital technology, some companies have created a new position in the "C-suite": Chief Marketing Technologist. The CMT's role is to set a vision for how the company will use marketing technology and lead the execution of that vision. Some companies have also created the role of Chief Content Officer, recognizing the growing importance of content in marketing and sales processes. Mattel, for example, has established an entirely new content division, Mattel Creations, under the direction of their Chief Content Officer.

CHANGING ROLE OF SALES

Defining a sales strategy in Third Digital requires taking into account the changing role of sales and salespeople within the customer journey. What matters is buying, not selling. Customers are buying differently, so companies need to be selling differently. Today's customers want to go further in the journey before engaging a salesperson. They prefer the convenience and accuracy of doing their own online research over dealing with a person. Companies that don't facilitate this by providing excellent digital touchpoints are at an ever-increasing disadvantage.

Sales strategy needs to be omnichannel in nature, redefining the role of each channel and each touchpoint, whether digital or human, so that the experience is smooth and seamless at every stage of the customer journey.

The real estate company Redfin is a good example of redefining sales strategy—in fact, their name is a derived from the word "Redefine." Traditional home real estate agents are responsible for creating leads and closing sales. However, Redfin realized that digital systems are better at generating leads. Redfin generates leads through content marketing, Search Engine Optimization, and personalized content. This approach is also consistent with most people's preference for engaging with a sales representative only later in the process. The digitally generated leads are handed to the sales agents, who are then responsible for helping the prospect through the sales process. Redfin agents rely on inside coordinators to help schedule the tours, so the agent spends the bulk of their time on the activities valued by the buyers: understanding their needs, showing them houses, and helping them through the transaction. Rather than being paid by commission, agents are compensated based on the number of house tours they provide, customer satisfaction, and sales.

This approach is new and interesting, but is it working? Well, they are a private company, so there is not much information available. What we do know is that they have captured 3.5% of the real estate transactions in Seattle, which is a sizable share for a twelve-year-old company in a giant industry.

Improving the journey also means having product available to deliver when the customer orders it. Therefore, effective sales forecasting is critical. Sales forecasting in Third Digital relies more and more on data science. Traditional forecasting relied on historical data and input from sales managers, and those forecasts were usually inaccurate. Since forecasts are used to plan, acquire, and allocate resources, inaccurate forecasts cause waste, missed opportunities, and most importantly, unsatisfied customers. To avoid those issues, companies can rely on cloud-based analytics engines like Aviso that load years of sales data and create predictive algorithms. The algorithms are self-tested by making "predictions" from the past, then testing to see whether the data supports it.

RingCentral, a company that provides cloud service to 350,000 customers, is using this approach. They recently went public and saw their stock rise 40% above the IPO price. Since they started using predictive algorithms, their sales forecasts have been "dead on," allowing them to operate more efficiently.[8]

Companies are starting to implement predictive ordering—again, to have product available when the customer orders it. Through computer learning and advanced algorithms, some companies can predict what individual customers, or groups of customers, might order. This approach simplifies ordering since the order is already prepared for the customer, and all they have to do is make adjustments and hit "send". At the aggregate level, predictive ordering allows a company to arrange resources and inventory to deliver anticipated orders faster.

Over time, we will see more "passive buying"—orders placed by a sensor in the item itself based on usage and the need to replenish. Amazon took a first step in this direction in the B2C space with its Dash buttons. While not entirely passive, Amazon's Dash buttons allow consumers to reorder products at the push of a button. You may, for example, put one of their Dash buttons somewhere near your bottle of Tide detergent. When the bottle is almost empty, you simply have to push the button, which processes an order for more Tide.

Amazon has developed the concept further with Amazon Dash Replenishment Service, a platform that allows connected devices to order goods when supplies are running low. For example, a pet food company could provide a pet food dispenser with a sensor that automatically reorders the pet food as required. Amazon is inviting companies to participate in the platform. Whirlpool and GE currently provide the service to automatically reorder detergent, as do Brother and Samsung, to automatically reorder ink and toner for printers, and Brita, whose water pitchers will automatically reorder filters. The customers get convenience; the companies get favored customer relationships and increased revenue.

Lead generation and management are now mostly digital. Companies are using digital marketing to generate leads and email management systems and marketing automation systems to nurture those leads. Enterprises that use marketing automation software to automate repetitive tasks, such as email responses, social media content, and lead nurturing, generate more leads and sales than companies that don't.

The Salesforce 2015 State of Sales report surveyed 2,300 sales leaders and found that analytics, mobile sales apps, and other sales technology are effective and on the rise:[9]

- High-performing sales teams are 3.5 times more likely than under-performing teams to use sales analytics.
- While 47% of companies currently use sales analytics, 74% expect to use analytics within the next year.
- High performers are four times more likely to be using mobile sales apps.
- High-performing teams use more technology, freeing up the sales reps to sell.

Recent SaaS companies are exemplars of lead generation and revenue growth success. Companies like Slack, Dropbox, Docusign, Xero, and Workday got to billion-dollar valuations in just a few years. As companies are moving to "as-a-Service" models, where recurring revenue is the name of the game, several sales metrics are becoming more common:

- Lead velocity rate (percentage growth in the number of leads month over month)
- Monthly Recurring Revenue (MRR)
- Churn (Lost customers)
- Annual Recurring Revenue (ARR)

- Annual Contract Value (ACV)
- Lifetime Value (LTV)
- Customer Acquisition Cost (CAC)

Investors in SaaS companies like to see a lead velocity rate of 15% per month. That may sound aggressive—and it is: looking at that growth on an annual basis works out to 535% a year! SaaS companies also look for substantial Annual Contract Values, more than $10,000 per month, to get to billion-dollar size businesses. Lifetime Value should be at least three times greater than Customer Acquisition Cost, and for each customer, Customer Acquisition Cost should be recovered in less than one year. Investors also tend to look for the "rule of 40," which holds that growth rate plus profit should equal at least 40%.

NEW CUSTOMER SERVICE

Post-sales service is not a separate area but a component of the overall customer journey. When done well, customer service in Third Digital contributes to customer engagement, brand status, brand loyalty, and revenue. That is why companies are migrating their customer service function from cost centers to customer advocacy and engagement centers. They are, correspondingly, moving from such measures as numbers of calls handled and average time per call to Net Promoter Score (how likely the customer is to recommend you), First Contact Resolution (percent of problems resolved with one contact), and Problem Resolution Time.

That is also why companies are striving for consistent messaging and experience across all channels and touchpoints. Effective customer service improvement programs look at all functions and how they impact customer service. Shipping, IT, and billing can impact customer service as much as the front-line service representatives.

An emerging practice, particularly for B2B companies, is to set up a customer success function, in addition to customer service. While the role of customer service is to support customers with post-purchase questions, defects, or problems, and is reactive in nature, the role of customer success is to help the customer achieve the desired outcome and is more proactive in nature. Customer success is intended to help the customer realize maximum value from the product. It requires knowing the individual customers and following them through their entire journey.

Social media enables customers to communicate their happiness or unhappiness loudly and extensively. Therefore, a large part of planning the customer service workforce in the digital world is staffing the social media monitoring and customer service teams.

In North America, GM has a staff of 26 full-time people who provide customer service via social media. The team works as part of a 600-person social Media Center of Expertise (COE) to provide service 16 hours per day, seven days per week, covering 6,000 interactions per month from customers and prospects.[10]

The CoE also conducts sentiment analysis. The following quote from Alicia Boler-Davis, Senior Vice President, Global Connected Customer Experience at GM, is a good example of the power of social media monitoring:

> "Recently, the team identified a faulty climate control part when a customer posted the issue on a product owner blog. After seeing the complaint receive dozens of replies and thousands of views, it was clear we needed to investigate further. The CoE elevated the issue to the engineering leads. Once the team determined the root cause of the problem, a technical service bulletin was released to all dealerships to replace the affected HVAC control modules on vehicles already built. We fixed the original customer's vehicle within 10 days, and beyond helping a customer who did not directly ask us for help, we also made adjustments in production to ensure no additional customers would be affected."[11]

In Third Digital, companies should have the ability to know as much or more about the condition of the product than the customer does. Sensors in products can alert the company and the customer about the troubled situation or a condition that may result in failure of the product.

The company may even have the opportunity to proactively reach out to the customer about a potential problem before it occurs.

Sensors, IoT, and big data can also be used to continuously improve the reliability of the product. Analyzing defects to learn when and where they occurred, and under what conditions, provides the insights necessary to improve the product. Better reliability contributes to better Net Promoter scores, regardless of how great the service interaction and actual service are.

Customer service also includes managing product recalls. IoT helps reduce incidents of recalls because products are more closely monitored and better fault data is produced, which can be used to engineer out defects. Increased digitization of manufacturing and the entire supply chain will reduce human error and thereby reduce recalls.

A single recall for an automotive company can cost $1 billion. In 2014, GM reported the cost of product recalls was $4.1 billion, including repair, victim compensation, and other expenses. The biggest component, at $2.8 billion, was the cost to repair. GM finished 2014 at break-even, showing that the cost of recalls wiped out their profits in a year in which they achieved sales records. Far more important, their flawed ignition switch problem was tied to 51 deaths.

Besides reducing the actual number of recalls, IoT can also help reduce the cost and danger of recalls when they do occur. If the repair can occur via the Internet, then the cost of repair is minuscule. In 2014, Tesla had a recall of 29,222 wall charger units which had the potential to overheat during charging. The remedy was to issue an over-the-air software update that would detect unexpected fluctuations in the input power—an indication of potential overheating—and reduce charging current to avoid overheating.[12]

While IoT will help decrease the number and cost of recalls, IoT unfortunately also opens up new risks in the area of cyber security. In 2015, Fiat Chrysler recalled 1.4 million cars because research showed that vehicle systems could be cyber attacked. Fiat Chrysler was able to address that vulnerability with a software update. On July 31, 2015, the Food and Drug Administration (FDA) advised hospitals to not use Hospira's Symbiq infusion system because it appeared that cyber attackers could take control of the devices.[13] The examples show that security must be a top priority for companies deploying IoT initiatives.

Companies are wrestling with the correct measures with which to assess customer service and customer satisfaction in the new digital era. Besides the Net Promoter Score and Customer Lifetime Value ratings discussed earlier, value sharing and customer engagement measures are becoming more common. For example, Apple measures and tracks the number of developers creating apps for iOS and the money generated by the apps for the Apple community. Zappos measures performance of customer service agents based on whether or not they made a personal connection with the caller.

Measuring customer satisfaction and sentiment should also point out where customers prefer human, rather than digital, interaction. Companies also need to be cautious about "over-digitizing" customer service. A study by Accenture discovered the following statistics:[14]

- 58% of customers prefer dealing with humans to get quick answers to questions.
- 73% prefer people for solving service issues.
- 73% seek out people for advice.
- 52% have switched providers in the past year due to poor customer service—83% of these said better live/in-person customer service would have impacted their decision.
- In the United States, the estimated cost of customers switching due to poor service is $1.6 trillion.

CONCLUSION

Helping customers get to their desired outcome quickly and pleasantly is an objective that requires ongoing and continuous improvement in the digital world. As companies improve, customer expectations increase, and companies are forced to meet higher standards. A continuous cycle.

Now that we have examined the components of digital transformation—vision, products, processes, customer journey—the next Chapter pulls these together into overall action.

Nine

Action Planning

Knowledge is not useful if it is not applied. This chapter applies the insights of the previous chapters to define and plan digital improvements. I suggest four steps:

1. Vision
2. Assessment
3. Initiative definition and business case
4. Initiative execution

The best approach is to execute these steps with a group of senior executives from the company. Alternatively, if a particular function or line of business is undertaking these exercises, a small group from that function or line of business should be assembled.

The worksheets presented in this chapter are available for download at *http://thirddigital.com*.

VISION

Chapter 5 described in detail how to establish a digital vision. Recall the framework used to assess the threats and opportunities. Squares 1, 5, and 6 of Figure 9-1 represent the greatest areas of threat or opportunity, depending on how you look at it. If your product (or service) is in one of these boxes, you are well-poised to become a disruptor—or to become disrupted if you ignore the digital opportunities. If you are in Square 1, embed digital technologies to improve your product. If you are in Square 5, leverage digital to lower your costs substantially. If you are in Square 6, use digital to make your customers' journey better. Understanding which square your key products or lines of business sit in will set the stage for your vision exercise. A good start is to write your products into the appropriate square in Figure 9-1.

	Digital Enables Product Improvements **Better**	Digital Enables Internal Process Improvements **Lower Cost**	Digital Enables Customer Process Improvements **Easier**
Differentiated Products	1. Disruption Likely	2. Disruption Possible	3. Disruption Possible
Commodity Products	4. Not Applicable	5. Disruption Likely	6. Disruption Likely

Figure 9-1: Opportunity Mapping

In Chapter 5, we looked at a set of questions to address when establishing your digital vision. These are reproduced in Table 9-1.

Products—Maximize the value	Processes—Minimize the cost and effort	Customer Journey—Minimize the cost and effort
What digital technology or information is valuable to customers and should be embedded into our products or provided as a service?	How do we minimize movement and automate processes and make them faster, more reliable, and lower cost?	How can digital make the customer processes, such as ordering, receiving, getting service, and using the products easier?

Table 9-1. Digital Vision Questions

Recall that for your company or for particular lines of business or products, one of the three questions above may be more important than the others. Also, these are starter questions only. As you establish your vision, you might use these questions, add to them, or come up with a different set. It does not matter. What matters is establishing some sort of vision that covers one or more of the three areas as a premise for your key digital initiatives.

DIGITAL SELF-ASSESSMENT

The second step is to do a self-assessment. Chapters 6, 7, and 8 provided ideas on how to improve products, operational processes, and the customer journey by leveraging digital technologies. You can use those chapters as a basis for evaluating the current digital state of your company.

Digital in Products

For your key products, assess the degree to which you are currently embedding digital for each of these areas. The sheet in Figure 9-2 can be used to indicate where your company is in each area (Not Started, Started, Advanced) and the business impact of advancing further (Low, Medium, High).

Embedding Digital into Products and Services	Current Assessment			Business Impact of Advancing		
	Not Started	Started	Advanced	Low	Med.	High
Embed digital to **monitor** our products						
Embed digital to **analyze** our products						
Adjust our products real-time and long-term						
Use product data to **recommend** better customer outcomes						

Figure 9-2: Digital in Product Worksheet

I suggest the following definitions for the Assessment columns:

- Not Started: For the product being assessed, we are not yet embedding digital.
- Started: We are somewhat embedding digital, but we are still in the early stages.
- Advanced: We are further along when compared to most of our competitors.

For the business impact of advancing, the intent is to assess the value of further digitizing products in that area. It is best to use a metric that is most valuable to your company and assign numbers. For example, your metric may be operating margin. You may define "Low" as less than $1 million in additional margin, "medium" as $1 to $10 million in additional margin, and "High" as more than $10 million in additional margin. Again, it is up to you and whatever is most relevant to your company.

Digital in Operational Processes

Chapter 7 gave examples of leading digital practices across operational processes, and you can download a complete set at *www.thirddigital. com*. To do the assessment, your team can refer to those examples for each process, using them as a reference. Based on the examples, check the appropriate column in the sheet in Figure 9-3, for Current Assessment and Business Impact of Addressing. (Ignore Potential Initiatives for now.) Consider the following definitions for Current Assessment:

- Not Started: For this process, we have not embarked on any digital initiatives like the ones described in Chapter 7 or the more complete set downloaded.
- Started: For this process, we have introduced some digital aspects.
- Advanced: For this process, we are further than most of our competitors, including startups and companies in other industries.

For the "Business Impact of Addressing" columns, I suggest the approach described above for the Product side.

Process	Current Assessment			Business Impact of Advancing			Potential Initiatives
	Not Started	Started	Ad-vanced	Low	Med-ium	High	
Deliver Physical Products and Services							
Plan for and align supply chain resources							
Procure materials and services							
Produce/Manufacture/Deliver product							
Manage logistics and warehousing							
Est. service delivery governance and strategies							
Manage service delivery resources							
Deliver service to customer							
Develop and Manage Human Capital							
Dev. and manage HR planning, policies, strat.							
Recruit, source, and select employees							
Develop and counsel employees							
Manage employee relations							
Reward and retain employees							
Redeploy and retire employees							
Manage employee information and analytics							
Manage employee communication							
Deliver employee communications							
Manage Information Technology (IT)							
Manage the business of information technology							
Develop and manage IT customer relationships							
Dev. and impl. security, privacy, data protection							
Manage enterprise information							
Develop and maintain IT solutions							
Deploy information technology solutions							
Deliver and support IT services							
Manage Financial Resources							
Perform planning and management accounting							
Perform revenue accounting							
Perform general accounting and reporting							
Manage fixed-asset project accounting							
Process payroll							
Process AP and expense reimbursements							
Manage treasury operations							
Manage internal controls							
Manage taxes							
Acquire, Construct, and Manage Assets							
Plan and acquire assets							
Design and construct productive assets							
Maintain productive assets							
Dispose of assets							
Manage Risk, Compliance, and Remediation							
Manage enterprise risk							
Manage compliance							
Manage remediation efforts							
Manage business resiliency							
Manage External Relationships							
Build investor relationships							
Manage government and industry relationships							
Manage relations with board of directors							
Manage legal and ethical issues							
Manage public relations program							
Develop and Manage Business Capabilities							
Manage business processes							
Manage portfolio, program, and project							
Manage enterprise quality							
Manage change							
Dev. and manage knowledge management							
Measure and benchmark							
Manage environmental health and safety (EHS)							

These processes are based on the APQC Process Classification Framework, which is an open stndard developed by APQC, a non-profit which promotes benchmarking and best practices worldwide. The PCF is intended to facilitate organizational improvement through process benchmarking, regardless of industry. size or geography. To download the full PCF, as well as associated measures and benchmarking. please visit www.apqc.org/pcf.

Figure 9-3: Digital in Process Worksheet

The purpose of scoring the digital state of the operational processes is to isolate where the opportunities are. Clearly, no company would embark on a journey to advance digitization on all or even a majority of processes at once. If you are doing the exercise for one function or process area, then you would complete the template only for that function.

Customer Journey Digital Assessment

The first step is to map out your customer's journey as described in Chapter 8. Then map it to your key marketing, sales and service processes to examine which process serves which step in the journey. Figure 9-4 provides an example for a Business to Consumer (B2C) company, and figure 9-5 is an example for a Business to Business (B2B) company. These are examples only. Yours will be different. In fact, you each may have different lines of business with different customer journeys.

Journey Step (Examples)	Outbound Marketing	Inbound Marketing	Sales	Customer Service
Recognize Need				
Become Aware of Solutions	✓			
Research		✓		
Decide			✓	
Order or Purchase			✓	
Receive				
Pay			✓	
Use				✓
Recommend				

Figure 9-4: B2C Customer Journey Map Worksheet Example

Journey Step (Examples)	Outbound Marketing	Inbound Marketing	Sales	Customer Service
Recognize Need				
Identify problem	✓			
Prepare business case			✓	
Research Solutions				
Search web		✓		
Consult colleagues		✓		
Develop shortlist of candidate solutions	✓	✓		
Decide				
Request proposals			✓	
Evaluate proposals			✓	
Meet with potential suppliers			✓	
Final negotiations			✓	
Order				
Get approval for the purchase			✓	
Prepare and issue purchase order			✓	
Receive and Pay				
Receive goods or services				
Issue goods receipt				
Approve invoice				
Pay invoice				
Use				
Install and set up, if applicable				✓
Train users				✓
Use product				✓
Maintain product				✓
Assess benefits against business case				
Recommend				
Act as a reference			✓	
Take inquiries				

Figure 9-5: B2B Customer Journey Map Worksheet Example

This mapping enables you to see if there are steps in the journey where you are not sufficiently helping the customer. In the B2C example above, it appears the customer is on their own at the Recognize Need and Recommend steps. The B2C company is not helping with the entire set of Receive and Pay steps, identifying potential new areas to help the customer.

Then, anywhere there is a checkmark, your team can ask two questions:

- How easy is the step now for the customer?
- How can digital make this step easier or eliminate the need for it altogether?

This exercise will generate additional digital initiatives for consideration.

At the risk of overusing Amazon as a B2C example, you can see how they continually ask those questions and take action to make things easier. They recommend products you might like (for the Become Aware of Solutions step); they provide one-click ordering (for the Order or Purchase step); and they offer one-hour delivery (for the Receive step).

Vision Review

After completing the self-assessment, your team may want to review the vision. Be sure to have cross-functional participation and buy-in in the digital vision, including all levels and all applicable business units and geographies of the organization. If your company is less advanced than you thought when you first formulated your vision, you may want to pull back a bit to make sure it is achievable. If your company is more advanced, your team may want to stretch the vision a little more.

INITIATIVE DEFINITION AND BUSINESS CASE

Customer journey improvements and product and process areas where advancing would have a high business impact are, of course, the top priority areas in which to establish initiatives. Based on the areas of high business potential, your team should identify initiatives that will advance that area (a single initiative may cover several areas).

The number of initiatives your company decides to undertake will depend on your company's capacity and vision. However, be aware that proceeding with digital transformation is not optional. Business is digital. The less progress you make, the more of your market you will hand over to more digitally aggressive competitors.

To ensure your company follows through with the planned initiatives, only those initiatives with a solid business case should proceed. The business world is littered with examples of large initiatives that failed or were aborted because there simply wasn't a strong enough reason—a clear and strong business case—to see them through to completion.

The business case does not need to be limited to numbers—sometimes a numeric Return on Investment is impossible to calculate. A clear understanding that an initiative will, for example, make the customer journey substantially better is sufficient.

INITIATIVE EXECUTION

The initiatives you identify form an overall digital transformation roadmap. The top executives must drive implementation of the roadmap. The CEO must not only buy into the vision and digital roadmap but actively communicate it and drive its execution. If your CEO does not believe that digital transformation is a top priority, convince them that it is. If you cannot, find a different place to work—at a company that will survive.

The entire company should be aware of and involved in executing the digital transformation roadmap. These initiatives are likely to touch every employee over the long run.

The execution plan must include necessary governance. Often, a digital transformation office is established to ensure performance and progress or a digital transformation steering committee is formed to direct the overall effort.

Your team will decide which execution approach works best for your company. One thing is sure: defining and executing the digital roadmap is not optional. Enterprises that understand the priority of digitizing and succeed at leveraging it to continuously improve products and processes are the ones that will thrive and drive value over the long term.

CONCLUSION

This chapter presented an approach to identifying digital priorities and initiatives, leveraging the other chapters of the book. These are exciting times for industrial companies to dive hard into digital. Those who do digital right will be the big winners in the third digital era. Enjoy the ride!

Appendix:

Companies Examined

Banks

Bank of America Corp., Bank of Montreal, Bank of Nova Scotia, BB&T Corp., BlackRock, BNY Mellon, Canadian Imperial Bank of Com., Citigroup Inc., Comerica Inc., Fifth Third Bancorp, Franklin Resources, Huntington Bancshares, JPMorgan Chase & Co., KeyCorp, Legg Mason, M&T Bank Corp., Northern Trust Corp., People's United Bank, PNC Financial SVCS Group Inc, Royal Bank of Canada, SunTrust Banks, Toronto-Dominion Bank, U.S. Bancorp, Wells Fargo, Zions Bancorp

Biotech and Pharma

Alexion Pharmaceuticals, Amgen Inc., Biogen Idec Inc., Celgene Corp., Eli Lilly and Co., Endo International plc, Gilead Sciences, Merck & Co., Mylan Inc., Perrigo, Pfizer Inc., Regeneron, Valeant Pharmaceuticals Int'l

Broadcasting and Communications

AT&T, BCE Inc., Cablevision Systems Corp., CBS, CenturyLink Inc., Comcast, Discovery Com, Level 3 Communications, Scripps Networks Int., TEGNA Inc, The Walt Disney Co., Thomson Reuters, Time Warner Cable Inc., Twenty-First Century Fox, Verizon Communications

Consumer Discretionary
Carnival Corp., Chipotle Mexican Grill, D. R. Horton, Darden Restaurants, Garmin Ltd., Hanesbrands Inc, Interpublic Group, Lennar Corp., Marriott International, McDonald's Corp., Michael Kors Holdings, Mohawk Industries, Newell Rubbermaid Co., Nike Inc., Omnicom Group, PulteGroup Inc, Royal Caribbean Cruises, Snap-On Inc., Stanley Black & Decker, Starbucks Corp., Starwood Hotels & Res, Tiffany & Co., Under Armour, V.F. Corp., Whirlpool Corp., Wyndham Worldwide, Yum! Brands Inc.

Consumer Packaged Goods
Altria Group Inc., Archer-Daniels-Midland Co., Brown-Forman Corp., Campbell Soup, Church & Dwight Co, Colgate-Palmolive, ConAgra Foods Inc., Constellation Brands, Dr Pepper Snapple Group, Estee Lauder Cos., General Mills Inc., Hasbro Inc., Hormel Foods Corp., J.M. Smucker Co., Kellogg, Kimberly-Clark, Mattel Inc., McCormick & Co., Molson Coors Brewing Co., Mondelez Int'l, Monster Beverage, PepsiCo Inc., Philip Morris Int'l, Procter & Gamble, Reynolds American Inc., The Clorox Company, The Coca Cola Co., Tyson Foods

Diversified Financial Services
American Express Co, Ameriprise Financial, Capital One Financial, Charles Schwab Corp., CME Group Inc., Discover Financial Services, E*Trade Financial Corp., Goldman Sachs Group, H&R Block Inc., Intercontinental Exchange, Leucadia National Corp., Moody's Corp, NASDAQ OMX Group, Principal Financial Group, Prologis, Prudential Financial, State Street Corp., T. Rowe Price Group, Unum Group, Ventas Inc.

Health Care Equipment & Distribution
Abbott Laboratories, Agilent Technologies Inc., Baxter International Inc., Becton Dickinson, Boston Scientific, Bristol-Myers Squibb, C. R. Bard Inc, Cardinal Health Inc., Cerner, Edwards Lifesciences, Express Scripts, Henry Schein Inc, Johnson & Johnson, McKesson Corp., Medtronic Inc.,

PerkinElmer, St. Jude Medical Inc., Stryker Corp., Thermo Fisher Scientific, Varian Medical Systems, Waters Corp., Zimmer Biomet Holdings

Health Care Providers
Aetna Inc., Anthem Inc., Cigna Corp., DaVita Inc., Dentsply Int'l, HCA Inc., Humana Inc., LabCorp, Patterson Companies, Quest Diagnostics, Tenet Healthcare Corp., United Health Group Inc., Universal Health Services

Industrials
3M Company, Advance Auto Parts Inc, Airgas Inc., Amphenol Corp., Boeing Co., BorgWarner Inc, C. H. Robinson Worldwide, Canadian National Railway, Canadian Pacific Railway, Caterpillar Inc., Cintas Corp., Corning Inc., CSX Corp., Danaher Corp., Deere & Co., Delta Air Lines, Dover Corp., Eaton Corporation, Emerson Electric Co, Expeditors Int'l, Fastenal Co., FedEx Corporation, FLIR Systems, Flowserve Corporation, Fluor Corp., Ford Motor, General Dynamics, General Electric, General Motors, Harley-Davidson, Honeywell Int'l Inc., Illinois Tool Works, Ingersoll-Rand PLC, J. B. Hunt Transport Services Inc., Jacobs Engineering Group, Johnson Controls, Kansas City Southern, L-3 Comm's Holdings, Leggett & Platt, Lockheed Martin Corp., Masco Corp., Norfolk Southern Corp., Northrop Grumman Corp., PACCAR Inc., Parker-Hannifin, Pentair Ltd., Pitney-Bowes, PotashCorp, Quanta Services Inc., Raytheon Co., Republic Services Inc., Robert Half International, Rockwell Automation Inc., Rockwell Collins, Roper Industries, Ryder System, Southwest Airlines, Stericycle Inc., Sysco Corp., Textron Inc., Tyco Int'l, Union Pacific, United Continental Holdings, United Parcel Service, United Technologies, Verisk Analytics Inc, W. W. Grainger Inc., Waste Management

Information Technology
Accenture plc, Activision Blizzard Inc, Adobe Systems Inc., Alliance Data Systems Corp., Analog Devices Inc., Applied Materials Inc., Autodesk Inc., Avago Technologies, CA Inc., Cisco Systems, Cognizant Technology Sol., Dun & Bradstreet, Electronic Arts, Expedia Inc., F5 Networks, First Solar Inc,

GameStop Corp., Harris Corp., Hewlett-Packard Co, IBM Corp., Intel Corp., Iron Mountain Inc., Juniper Networks, KLA-Tencor Corp., Lam Research, Linear Technology Corp., Microchip Technology, Micron Technology, Motorola Solutions Inc., Nielsen Holdings, Nvidia Corp., Priceline.com Inc, Qualcomm Inc., Red Hat Inc., SanDisk Corporation, Seagate Technology, Skyworks Solutions Inc., Symantec Corp., TE Connectivity Ltd., Teradata Corp., Texas Instruments, Western Digital, Xerox Corp., Xilinx Inc.

Insurance
AFLAC Inc., AIG Inc., Allstate Corp., Aon plc, Assurant Inc., Berkshire Hathaway, Chubb, Cincinnati Financial, Great-West Lifeco, Hartford Financial Services, Lincoln National, Loews, Manulife Financial, Marsh & McLennan, MetLife Inc., Progressive Corp., The Travelers Companies, Torchmark Corp., XL Capital

Internet Commerce and Services
ADP LLC., Akamai Technologies Inc., Alphabet Inc. Class A, Amazon.com Inc., Citrix Systems, Fidelity Nat. Info. Services, Fiserv Inc, Intuit Inc., Mastercard Inc., NetApp, Netflix Inc., Paychex Inc., Salesforce.com, Total System Services, TripAdvisor, Verisign Inc., Visa Inc., Western Union Co., Yahoo Inc.

Materials
Air Products & Chemicals, Alcoa Inc., Avery Dennison Corp, Ball Corp, CF Industries Holdings Inc., Dow Chemical, Eastman Chemical, Ecolab, Freeport-McMoRan Inc., International Paper Co., Intl Flavors & Fragrances, LyondellBasell, Martin Marietta Materials, Newmont Mining Corp., Nucor Corp., Owens-Illinois Inc., PPG Industries, Praxair Inc., Sherwin-Williams Co., The Mosaic Co., Vulcan Materials, WestRock Co.

Oil & Gas
Anadarko Petroleum Corp., Apache Corporation, Baker Hughes Inc., Cabot Oil & Gas, Canadian Natural Resources, Chesapeake Energy, Chevron, Cimarex Energy, ConocoPhillips, Devon Energy Corp., Diamond Offshore

Drilling, Enbridge, Ensco plc, EOG Resources, EQT Corporation, Exxon Mobil, FMC Technologies Inc., Halliburton Co., Helmerich & Payne, Hess Corporation, Husky Energy, Imperial Oil, Marathon Oil Corp., Marathon Petroleum, Murphy Oil, Newfield Exploration Co., Noble Energy Inc., ONEOK Inc., Pioneer Natural Resources, Range Resources Corp., Schlumberger Ltd., Southwestern Energy, Spectra Energy Corp., Suncor Energy, Tesoro Petroleum Co., Transcanada, Transocean, Valero Energy, Williams Companies

Real Estate and REITs
Aimco, American Tower Corp., AvalonBay Communities, Boston Properties, CBRE Group, Crown Castle Int'l Corp., Essex Property Trust Inc., General Growth Properties, HCP Inc., Host Hotels & Resorts, Kimco Realty, Macerich, Public Storage, Realty Income Corporation, Simon Property Group Inc., SL Green Realty Corp, Vornado Realty Trust, Weyerhaeuser Corp.

Retail
AutoNation Inc., AutoZone Inc., Bed Bath & Beyond, Best Buy Co. Inc., Carmax Inc., Costco Co., CVS Health, Dollar General, Dollar Tree, Gap Inc., Genuine Parts, Goodyear Tire & Rubber, Kroger Co., L Brands Inc., Lowe's Cos., Macy's Inc., Nordstrom, O'Reilly Automotive, Ross Stores, Signet Jewelers Limited, Staples Inc., Target Corp., TJX Companies Inc., Tractor Supply Co., United Rentals Inc., Walgreens Boots Alliance, Wal-Mart Stores, Whole Foods Market

Utilities
AES Corp., AGL Resources Inc., Ameren Corp., American Electric Power, CenterPoint Energy, CMS Energy, Consolidated Edison, Dominion Resources, DTE Energy Co., Duke Energy, Edison Int'l, Entergy Corp., Eversource Energy, Exelon Corp., FirstEnergy, NextEra Energy, NiSource Inc., NRG Energy, PG&E Corp., Pinnacle West Capital, PPL Corp., Public Serv. Enterprise Inc., SCANA Corp., Sempra Energy, Southern Co., WEC Energy Group Inc, Xcel Energy Inc.

Notes

Part 1: Understanding the Digital World

Chapter 1: The Digital World

1. Ceruzzi, Paul E. *A History of Modern Computing*. London, Eng.: MIT, 2003. 32-34. Print.

2. General Electric. *2006 annual report of General Electric*. Retrieved from http://www.ge.com/ar2006/pdf/ge_ar2006_full_book.pdf.

Chapter 2: Digital and Corporate Performance

1. Rogers, R.K. and Grant, J. (1997), "An empirical investigation of the relevance of the financial reporting process to financial analysts," Unpublished manuscript, Portland State University, February.

2. Smith, M., and Taffler, R.J. (2000) "The chairman's statement—A content analysis of discretionary narrative disclosures." Accounting, Auditing & Accountability Journal, 13(5), pp. 624–647. doi: 10.1108/09513570010353738.

Chapter 3: Key Technologies—First and Second Digital

1. Glazer, Emily. "J.P. Morgan Creates Executive Role to Lead Cloud Services." *The Wall Street Journal*. Dow Jones & Company, 24 Aug. 2016. Web. 02 Dec. 2016.

2. Kemp, Simon. "Digital in 2016 - We Are Social." We Are Social. N.p., Jan. 27, 2016. Web. Sept. 29, 2016.

3. Mell, Peter, and Timothy Grance. "The NIST Definition of Cloud Computing." (n.d.): n. pag. Http://nvlpubs.nist.gov/. The National Institute of Standards and Technology, Sept. 2011. Web.

Chapter 4: Key Technologies—Third Digital

1. Mercer, Margi Murphy & Christina. "These Companies Are Using Watson Big Data and Analytics to Power Their Business." ComputerworldUK. Computerworld, July 25, 2016. Web. Sept. 29, 2016.

2. "What Is IBM Watson?" IBM Watson: What Is Watson? IBM, n.d. Web. Sept. 29, 2016.

3. "Ten Years of Google Translate." Official Google Blog. Google, Apr. 28, 2016. Web. Sept. 29, 2016.

4. Wakefield, Jane. "Intelligent Machines: The Jobs Robots Will Steal First." BBC News. N.p., Sept. 14, 2015. Web. Sept. 29, 2016.

5. Ford, Martin. Rise of the Robots: Technology and the Threat of a Jobless Future (p. 4). Basic Books. Kindle Edition.

6. Garfield, Leanna. "7 Companies That Are Replacing Human Jobs with Robots." Tech Insider. N.p., 26 Feb. 2016. Web. Sept. 29, 2016.

7. Kalacota, Ravi. "Robotic Process Automation + Analytics." Business Analytics 30. N.p., May 16, 2016. Web. Sept. 29, 2016.

8. Frey, Carl Benedikt, and Michael A. Osborne. "The Future of Employment: How Susceptible Are Jobs to Computerization." University of Oxford (2013): n. pag. Web. 6 Dec. 2016.

Part Two: How to Thrive in Digital

1. "About APQC." About APQC. APQC, n.d. Web. Sept. 14, 2016

2. "Process Classification Framework | APQC." Process Classification Framework | APQC. APQC, n.d. Web. Sept. 14, 2016.

Chapter 5: Setting Your Digital Vision

1. "Publishing." Wikipedia. Wikimedia Foundation, n.d. Web. Sept. 29, 2016.

Chapter 6: Adding Digital to Products

1. Kim, W. Chan, and Renee Mauborgne. "Identify Blue Oceans by Mapping Your Product Portfolio." *Harvard Business Review*, Feb. 12, 2015. Web. Sept. 15, 2016.

2. Torres, Timothy. "The Best Smart Light Bulbs of 2016." *PC Magazine* May 31, 2016: n. pag. Web. Sept. 14, 2016.

3. Johnston, Hillary. "6 Best Electronic Door Locks for Your Home." SafeWise.com, Aug. 18, 2016. Web. Sept. 14, 2016.

4. Martin, James A. "10 'Smart Luggage' Options for Tech-savvy Travelers." CIO. CIO, July 10, 2015. Web. Sept. 14, 2016.

5. Weinswig, Deborah. "The Disruptors of Sports: Smart Sports Equipment." Fung Global Retail & Technology (2016): n. pag. June 14, 2016. Web. Sept. 14, 2016.

6. Kasten, Matt. "Babolat Play Connected Tennis Racket Is the Future of Tennis." SportTechie. Sporttechie.com, Feb. 9, 2015. Web. Sept. 14, 2016.

7. Adams, By Derek. "Digital Parenting: The Best Baby Tech and Connected Baby Monitors." Wearable. Wearable.com, Aug. 16, 2016. Web. Sept. 14, 2016.

8. "Smart Home Retrofit | 2016 Guidebook." Smart Home Retrofit | 2016 Guidebook. Postscapes.com, n.d. Web. Sept. 14, 2016.

9. "June Oven." June Intelligent Oven • The Computer-based Oven That Thinks like a Chef. June Life, Inc., n.d. Web. Sept. 14, 2016.

10. "Improving Downtime and Energy Efficiency with IoT Air Compressor." Intel. N.p., n.d. Web. Sept. 14, 2016.

11. "Experience the Smart Office Building." Intel. N.p., n.d. Web. Sept. 14, 2016

12. Dempsey, Michael. "Smart Containers Are Just the Start: How Connected Assets Will Drive the Digital Supply Chain Revolution." ORBCOMM. N.p., May 24, 2016. Web. Sept. 14, 2016; andBurnson, Patrick. "' 'Smart' Containers Signal Another New Trend." Recently Filed RSS. Logistics Management, Mar. 13, 2015. Web. Sept. 14, 2016.

13. Columbus, Louis. "IDC's Top 10 Manufacturing Predictions For 2016: The Cloud Enables Greater Customer Centricity." Forbes. *Forbes Magazine*, 19 Dec. 2015. Web. 06 Dec. 2016.

Chapter 7 Digitizing Operational Processes

1. "Industry 4.0 How to Navigate Digitization of the Manufacturing Sector." McKinsey Digital (2015): n. pag. Mckinsey.com. 2015. Web. 6 Dec. 2016.

2. "The Deloitte Global CPO Survey. Procurement: At a Digital Tipping Point." The Deloitte Global CPO Survey 2016 (n.d.): n. pag. Deloitte, 2016. Web. Aug. 20, 2016.

3. "IFR Press Release." IFR RSS. International Federation of Robotics, June 22, 2016. Web. Aug. 12, 2016

4. Yangon, Jiaxing And. "A Tightening Grip: Rising Chinese Wages Will Only Strengthen Asia's Hold on Manufacturing." The Economist (2015): n. pag. Web. 15 Jan. 2017.

5. "World Economic Forum White Paper Digital Transformation of Industries: Logistics." (2016): 17. Weforum.org. Web. Aug. 18, 2016.

6. Hern, Alex. "DHL Launches First Commercial Drone 'parcelcopter' Delivery Service." *The Guardian*. Guardian News and Media, Sept. 25, 2014. Web. Aug. 18, 2016.

7. Press Release. DHL. N.p., May 9, 2016. Web. Aug. 18, 2016. <http://www.dhl.com/en/press/releases/releases_2016/all/parcel_ecommerce/successful_trial_integration_dhl_parcelcopter_logistics_chain.html>.

8. Engelking, Carl. "Drone Delivery Services Are Booming In China—Drone 360." Drone 360. N.p., Mar. 27, 2015. Web. Aug. 18, 2016. <http://blogs.discovermagazine.com/drone360/2015/03/27/drone-delivery-china/#.V7YWwpgrJEY>.

9. Hall-Geisler, Kristen. "Google Gets a Patent for an Autonomous Delivery Truck." *Popular Science*. N.p., Feb. 18, 2016. Web. Aug. 18, 2016.

10. Parker, Samara. "7 Social Recruitment Stats & How to Apply Them." Jobcast.net. N.p., Mar. 23, 2015. Web. Sept. 29, 2016.

11. Medved, JP. "Top 15 Recruiting Statistics for 2014." Capterra Blog Comments. N.p., Feb. 20, 2014. Web. Sept. 29, 2016.

12. Galer, Susan. "Study: Employees Lack Skills for Digital Transformation." News.sap.com. SAP, Jan. 12, 2016. Web. Sept. 16, 2016.

13. Watt, Cecilia Saixue. "Will Digital Tech Create a New Labor Movement?—Techonomy." Techonomy. Techonomy, Aug. 10, 2015. Web. Sept. 16, 2016.

14. Isson, Jean Paul, and Jesse Harriott. *People Analytics in the Era of Big Data: Changing the Way You Attract, Acquire, Develop, and Retain Talent.* Hoboken: Wiley, 2016. N. pag. Print.

15. "Annual Study of Intangible Asset Market Value." Ocean Tomo. N.p., Mar. 5, 2015. Web. Aug., 15 2016.

16. Cox, David B. "Digital Transformation of the End-to-End Maintenance Lifecycle - Electronic Work Package." Accenture (2016): n. pag. Web. 6 Dec. 2016.

17. Rezendes, Christopher J., and W. Stephenson David. "Cyber Security in the Internet of Things." *Harvard Business Review.* Aug. 12, 2014. Web. Sept. 19, 2016.

18. Worstall, Tim, 1. "Stuxnet Was a Joint US/ Israeli Project." *Forbes Magazine.* June 1, 2012. Web. Sept. 19, 2016.

19. Penn-Hall, Luke. "The Blurring Line Between Cyber and Physical Threats." thecipherbrief.com. The Cipher Brief, Aug. 21, 2016. Web. Sept. 19, 2016.

20. Armerding, Taylor. "Top 15 Security Predictions for 2016." CSO Online. CSO, Apr. 15, 2016. Web. Sept. 19, 2016.

21. DiPietro, Ben. "Financial Firms Turn to Artificial Intelligence to Handle Compliance Overload." *The Wall Street Journal.* May 19, 2016. Web. Oct. 22, 2016.

22. Case, Steve. *The Third Wave: An Entrepreneur's Vision of the Future* (Kindle Locations 1648-1649). Simon & Schuster. Kindle Edition.

23. Bussey, Peter. "Harness Big Data & Predictive Analytics to Improve EHS Performance." LNS Research, Apr. 10, 2016. Web. Sept. 29, 2016.

24. Klee, Ann R. "The Digital Transformation of Environment, Health, and Safety." Home Page. Environmental Law Institute, Mar. 2016. Web. Sept. 27, 2016.

Chapter 8 Improving the Customer Journey

1. Sweetwood, Adel K. "How One Company Used Data to Rethink the Customer Journey" (2016): n. pag. Web. Aug. 24, 2016.

2. Edelman, David C., and Mark Singer. "Competing on Customer Journeys." *Harvard Business Review*, Aug. 4, 2016. Web. Oct. 20, 2016.

3. Bliss, Jeanne. *Chief Customer Officer 2.0: How to Build Your Customer-Driven Growth Engine* (Kindle Locations 1809-1829). Wiley. Kindle Edition.

4. "Digital Disconnect in Customer Engagement–Accenture." Digital Disconnect in Customer Engagement–Accenture. Accenture, n.d. Web. Aug. 23, 2016. <https://www.accenture.com/us-en/insight-digital-disconnect-customer-engagement>.

5. Hiner, Jason. "3 Things You Can Learn from the NFL about Digital Transformation." ZDNet (2016): n. pag. Zdnet.com. ZDNet, Aug. 29, 2016. Web. Aug. 29, 2016;Maddox, Teena. "How the NFL and Its Stadiums Became Leaders in Wi-Fi, Monetizing Apps, and Customer Experience." Tech Republic (2016): n. pag. Tech Republic. Web. 29 Aug. 2016.

6. Mooman, Christine. "CMO Survey Report: Highlights and Insights." (n.d.): n. pag. Web. Aug. 21, 2016. <https://cmosurvey.org/wp-content/uploads/sites/11/2016/02/The_CMO_Survey-Highlights_and_Insights-Feb-2016.pdf>.

7. Leone, Chris. "[Report] Inbound Vs. Outbound Marketing Budgets." [Report] Inbound Vs. Outbound Marketing Budgets. Web Strategies, 8 July 2016. Web. 06 Dec. 2016.

8. Wainewright, Phil. "Predictive Analytics Aids Sales Forecast Accuracy at RingCentral." Diginomica, Sept. 19, 2014. Web. Aug. 24, 2016.

9. Salesforce. "2015 State of Sales." Salesforce, n.d. Web. Aug. 24, 2016.

10. Boler-Davis, Alici. "How GM Uses Social Media to Improve Cars and Customer Service." *Harvard Business Review*, Feb. 12, 2016. Web. Sept. 15, 2016.

11. Isidore, Chris, 4. "GM's Total Recall Cost: $4.1 Billion." CNNMoney. Cable News Network, Feb. 4, 2015. Web. Sept. 16, 2016.

12. Blanco, Sebastian. "Tesla Recalling 29,000 Model S Wall Chargers to Prevent Overheating." Autoblog. Autoblog, Jan. 14, 2014. Web. Sept. 16, 2016.

13. "The Internet of Things Is Entering a Post-Recall Reality." *The Security Ledger*, Sept. 4, 2015. Web. Sept. 16, 2016.

14. "Digital Disconnect in Customer Engagement—Accenture." Digital Disconnect in Customer Engagement—Accenture, n.d. Web. Sept. 16, 2016.

Index

Software as a Service
(SaaS), 42, 103
subscription fees, 43
computer learning, 94
computer vision, 45, 55–56
Costco, 21
costs, positive impact of new
technology on, 45, 46
customer experience, digital
impact on
customer feedback, utiliz-
ing, 119
Customer Success teams,
119
demographics, studying,
119
expectations, rising, 118–9
physical companies, dis-
advantages to, 119
WiFi availability, 118
customer journey improvements,
5, 66–67, 134–36. See also
journey mapping
customer service, digital impact
on
consistent messaging,
importance of, 125
customer advocacy and
engagement centers,
move to, 125
customer success func-
tion, establishment of,
125–26

demographics to individ-
ual needs, move from,
117–18
examples, successful,
126–27
First Contact Resolution,
move to, 125
impact from other func-
tions, 125
importance of, 125
Net Promotor Score, move
to, 125, 127
over-digitizing, risk of, 128
post-sale, 125
Problem Resolution Time,
125
product condition, knowl-
edge of, 126
product recalls, 127
social media monitoring,
126
staffing, 126
value sharing and custom-
er engagement, 128

D
delivery service, digital impact on,
79
autonomous vehicles, 79,
97–98
cost and time reduction,
79
drones, 97, 79

product recalls, success-
ful, 127
RFID, 48, 49
security risk, increased,
107–8, 127
sending and receiving
data, 47–48
sensors, use of, 22–23, 47,
48–49, 127

J
journey mapping
B2B vs B2C companies,
114, 134
examples, 114–15, 116–17,
134–36
improving customer jour-
ney, 115
Moment of Truth (MoT)
priorities, 117
pricing strategies, 116
stages of customer jour-
ney, identifying,
114–15
value proposition, 115–16
JPMorgan Chase, 21, 37–38

K
Klee, Ann, 112
KPMG, 58

L
Lowes, 57

M
machine learning. *See also*
Google, Translate; IBM
banking and financial
uses, 52, 54, 105–6
benefits of leveraging, 4
big data analysis, 52–54
commercial uses for,
52–53, 54
digital initiatives, key
player in, 45
introduction and growth
of, 7, 12, 51–52
medical uses for, 52–53
security, 54
machine vision, 7, 12, 111
manufacturing, digital impact on
analytics for improving efficiency, 21
cost reductions, 95
machine learning, 54
maintenance, preventa-
tive vs predictive, 89,
95–96, 106
offshoring to cybershor-
ing, move from, 95
Overall Equipment
Effectiveness, 112
robotics, use of, 95, 111
Manulife, 21
marketing, digital impact on. *See
also* customer journey improvements; journey mapping

analytics, 120
budget allocation and
spending, 119–20
Chief Content Office, creation of, 121
Chief Marketing
Technologist (CMT),
creation of, 121
email campaigns, 120, 121
machine learning, 54
marketing automation
software, 124
mobile technology, 52,
120
outbound vs inbound, 121
social media, 120, 124
traditional advertising to
digital, 119–20, 121
Marsh & McLennan, 22
Mattel, 121
meal service, digital impact on, 80
microchips, 109
Microsoft, 11, 36
X-Box and Kinect, 55
MIT, 59
mobile technologies. *See also*
Apps
customer service and ex-
perience uses, 21, 23
digital initiatives, key
player in, 20, 26
health uses, 23

introduction and growth
of, 7
manufacturing uses, 21
mobile banking, 37
mobile phones, 36, 38–39,
84
personal computers, 39
sales uses, 124
tablets, 39, 106

N
nanobots, 12, 20, 45
Narrative Science, 55
natural language processing (NPL)
data analysis, 55
digital initiatives, key
player in, 12, 45
financial uses, 105–6
introduction and growth
of, 54–55
journalism uses, 55
security uses, 108
sentiment analysis, 55
speech recognition tech-
nology, 54
Nest, 88
Neurio, 88
Nike, 71–72

O
O'Neil, Cathy, 99
operational processes, digital
developments in

production and supply
chain, 94
self-assessing use of,
132–34
Osborne, Roddy F., 3
Oxford University, 59

P
Parker Hannifin, 22
Pay per Click, 121
Pitney Bowes, 72–73
PPL Corporation, 23
Product as a Service (PaaS). *See
also* cloud computing
data collection and analysis, 91–92
move toward, 92
products, digital-only, 67
programming language, 9, 10, 36
project management, digital
impact on
business optimization vs
business innovation,
110
change management, 110
Chief Digital Officer
(CDO), 110–11
Waterfall to Agile, shift
from, 110
public relations, digital impact on,
109

Q
Quiet Logistics, 57

R
radar, 109
Redfin, 122
robotics
agriculture, 56, 79
automobile industry leveraging, 12, 95
big data, 57–58
cost reductions from, 95
cybershoring vs offshor-
ing, 95
delivery, 79
digital initiatives, key
player in, 20, 45
employment, impact on,
59, 95
innovative uses for, 23
International Federation of
Robots (IFR), 95
introduction and growth
of, 7, 56–58
manufacturing, 13–14, 56,
80, 95–96
medical uses, 58
ransomware, 107–8
robotic process automa-
tion (RPA), 7, 12–13,
57–58, 104–5
Rogers, Rodney K., 19–20
Royal Caribbean Cruises, 23, 57

Wells Fargo, 37
Wilson, 87

X
Xerox, 91

Y
Yahoo, 20

Z
Zappos, 128

About the Author

Louis Lamoureux is a management consultant who helps companies use information technology to drive success. He was a Partner at Ernst & Young and at Deloitte Consulting, and he is the founder of Third Digital Inc., a firm dedicated to helping companies win big in the new digital era. As an entrepreneur, he has founded and managed several successful software companies." He holds BMath and MBA degrees. Louis lives in Chicago with his wife and children.